ROUTLEDGE LIBRARY EDITIONS:
SOCIOLOGY OF EDUCATION

Volume 52

CULTURE, EDUCATION AND THE STATE

CULTURE, EDUCATION AND THE STATE

Edited by
MICHAEL D. STEPHENS

Routledge
Taylor & Francis Group

LONDON AND NEW YORK

First published in 1988 by Routledge, Chapman and Hall

This edition first published in 2017
by Routledge
2 Park Square, Milton Park, Abingdon, Oxon OX14 4RN

and by Routledge
711 Third Avenue, New York, NY 10017

Routledge is an imprint of the Taylor & Francis Group, an informa business

British Library Cataloguing in Publication Data
A catalogue record for this book is available from the British Library

ISBN: 978-0-415-78834-2 (Set)
ISBN: 978-1-315-20949-4 (Set) (ebk)
ISBN: 978-1-138-62920-2 (Volume 52) (hbk)
ISBN: 978-1-138-62925-7 (Volume 52) (pbk)

Publisher's Note
The publisher has gone to great lengths to ensure the quality of this reprint but points out that some imperfections in the original copies may be apparent.

Disclaimer
The publisher has made every effort to trace copyright holders and would welcome correspondence from those they have been unable to trace.

Culture, Education and the State

Edited by
Michael D. Stephens

ROUTLEDGE

For Margaret Heap

First published in 1988 by
Routledge
a division of Routledge, Chapman and Hall
11 New Fetter Lane, London EC4P 4EE

© 1988 Michael D. Stephens

Printed and bound in Great Britain by
Biddles Ltd, Guildford and King's Lynn

British Library Cataloguing in Publication Data

Culture, education and the state.
 1. Great Britain. Cultural institutions
 I. Stephens, Michael D. (Michael Dawson),
 1936–
 941

 ISBN 0-415-01261-9

CONTENTS

Introduction: The State and Cultural Education
Michael D. Stephens   vii

1   The Arts Council
    David Jones   1

2   The British Council
    Paul Fordham with Warren Shaw   24

3   The British Library
    Kenneth Cooper   40

4   The British Museum
    John Reeve   65

5   The BBC
    Neil Barnes and John Cain   94

6   The Civic Trust and Amenity Societies
    Ray Banks   113

7   The Insite Trust. Places, Persons and the
    Professional: Learning and Teaching for
    Heritage
    Marista M. Leishman   130

8   Conclusion: Culture, Education and the State
    Kenneth Lawson   150

Contributors   164
Index   169

Introduction

THE STATE AND CULTURAL EDUCATION

Michael D. Stephens

Much of the second book of Benvenuto Cellini's autobiography concerns the author's relationship with Francis I of France. It is full of practical details of a major artist's working relationships in Sixteenth Century Europe

> On our way to the lodgings of the King we passed before those of the Cardinal of Ferrara. Standing at his door, he called to me and said: 'Our most Christian monarch has of his own accord assigned you the same appointments which his Majesty allowed the painter Leonardo da Vinci, that is, a salary of seven hundred crowns; in addition, he will pay you for all the works you do for him; also for your journey hither he gives you five hundred golden crowns, which will be paid you before you quit this place'. At the end of this announcement, I replied that those were offers worthy of the great King he was.

When modern governments act as if the state giving funding to cultural matters is a recent innovation, and perhaps should be transferred to the private sector, it is worth reminding ourselves that throughout most of history it has been the state, in the form of kings, or emperors, or city fathers, which has sustained both great art and important cultural events. Such contributions of often unequalled richness were always expensive, whether masques at the Court of Elizabeth I of England or the Athenian city-state building programme of the fifth century BC. Only those who controlled the state could be expected to command the necessary resources. Of course private individuals might also have substantial wealth to support the cultural life of their communities, even before the Industrial Revolution produced a much wider distribution of affluence. However, the state has invariably been the major factor in the cultural education of its citizens.

This substantial tradition needs to be remembered during the often heated debates which take place in most modern societies over the role, or lack of it, of the state in the cultural life of such communities. In Britain of recent years the dominant theme seems to have been how to save money. This is a simpler debate than those related to how a state should dispense its resources if it decides to take an interest in cultural sponsorship. To take one example the phenomenal loss of works of art to other countries during the Thatcher years demonstrates how low a priority recent British Administrations have given the subject of this book.

In modern states there are variations of three major models of state funding of cultural activities. There is the Ministry of Culture model such as that of Italy and West Germany. This assumes an interested, active, and policy making approach. It must imply more money from the government as there is a cabinet minister fighting for resources. The second model is that favoured by the British Government where a quango is set-up to distribute whatever money the cabinet decides to allocate. Whilst, at least in theory, this curbs the government's influence on how the money is spent it gives such fields as the arts a low spending priority. The final major model is that where private spending on cultural matters is encouraged by major tax concessions. This has met with considerable success in the United States and there is some support for implementing such legislation in Britain. The problem is that of judging the benefits in a country which lacks America's vast pool of very wealthy people. Whilst we should expect wealthy companies and individuals in states like Britain to support our cultural life they are not numerous enough to supplant the state as the major source of sponsorship. They are an important supplementary contribution.

For a country of Britain's rich cultural heritage and dynamic contemporary scene the ideal arrangement is probably to combine two of the above models and have a Minister of Culture and a tax system which encouraged companies and private individuals to buy paintings, sponsor concerts and theatre, give college scholarships, put up notable buildings, and a million other activities which educate our citizens into the unparalleled riches which can be made available to them.

The chapters which follow are built around the trio of inter-related themes of 'The State', 'Culture', and 'Education'. In the concluding chapter Kenneth Lawson deals with these words in the most direct manner as befits a philosopher, but other contributors handle them in a variety of ways which reflect both their own outlook and the particular qualities of the institutions they are writing about. There are usually more points in common than differences, but it would be surprising if the view from, say, the British Museum exactly paralleled that of the Nottingham Civic Trust. The encouragement of such diversity was intentional to illustrate the complexity of such a subject in a modern state. Things were simpler in fifteenth-century Florence. That does not mean that they were necessarily easier.

The case studies have been carefully chosen. Some seemed unavoidable if cultural education in a contemporary country was to be seriously considered, such as the inclusion of the BBC. Others had a distinctive quality about them which illustrated an original approach to rather new appetites. The British Council, with its brief to project British culture overseas, has a function which would have seemed more than novel to our grandparents' generation, for example. I have included a chapter on The Insite Trust as it is not strictly part of the state's cultural education contribution, being largely funded from other than governmental sources.

First and foremost the chapters are exercises in information giving. They are full of descriptions of the work of the institutions concerned. As funding is a central obsession of cultural education such descriptions do remind us of the high return achieved for each pound of governmental money invested. So often the tax-payers' pound triggers other contributions. A recent contract my University Department received from the British Council usefully demonstrates this. We have been granted £19,500 to send academics to advise in China over a three year period. The sum of £6,500 in a year will pay the travel and accommodation costs of one academic for a term and perhaps three others for much shorter periods. A very hard-pressed University has agreed to pay the salaries of the academics concerned when they are in Jinan, which is the first further contribution the British Council initiative has produced. In our initial advice we proposed that the Chinese should establish an Institute of Adult Education at Jinan to train teachers of adults and introduce modern research methods into China. With the confirmation that we were able to send advisers to Jinan the Shandong Provincial Government has agreed to fund such an Institute and its administrative staff have been appointed. Money has been allocated for 20 academic posts, with 50 more promised. The Institute will be one of three national centrès and is expected to transform the way China approaches the educational needs of its adult population. By its very modest investment the British Council will have notable influence on China's views of Britain and its culture.

Although there are doubters there is much evidence to suggest that cultural diplomacy results in goodwill towards the country concerned. An exhibition such as that in Washington in 1985-6 on the great houses of Britain ('The Treasure Houses of Britain', November 3, 1985 - March 16, 1986) educates Americans into aspects of British design and has had very practical outcomes. Japanese contacts have made me aware of the vast range of their design outside of the normal purchases of electrical goods I would make. We must not think only of the state and cultural education within one country, but also between countries.

The institutions here discussed do much to set our national cultural agenda, as David Jones points out in his description of the hugely influential Arts Council. By its funding the Arts Council can promote a cultural field, and by its neglect push another into near oblivion. It has looked after the citizens of London, but done little for the tax-payers of Nottingham. It has emphasised the culture of the past, but not been as effective in supporting the promotion of modern achievement.

A more complex society expects its cultural institutions to take on a broader educational role in return for whatever money the state allocates. As Kenneth Cooper's chapter shows, a foundation like a library is no longer seen as just a concentration of resources. The book is the artefact and from that base the library offers ever more services ranging from publishing, research, and the appointment of education officers to having an overseas development policy.

There is often a tension between the institution and its cultural education role. Whilst an increasingly utilitarian school curriculum, as John Reeve reminds us, gives agencies such as museums and art galleries a growing, supplementing, cultural education role this can challenge the assumption that their main focus is as collections of masterpieces.

Ray Banks states at one point in his essay 'We should not too readily mistrust our natural reactions to a proposed scheme'. Since 1945 in Britain there has frequently been a loss of self-confidence amongst the general public. The age of the professional has dawned with a vengeance and the cry of abuse 'Amateur!' has been heard throughout the land. In various areas of our cultural life the public has been told that it lacks the technical sophistication to make a judgement. Interestingly it is in that most accessible of the areas, architecture, that the most effective challenging of this professional viewpoint has arrived. In other areas such as music our fellow citizens have shown a dangerous indifference. As a result there is some cause for concern that musical composition has in Britain got itself up a bit of a technical back-alley. The general public cannot be educated to the level of technical sophistication of a professional musician, so a composer has an obligation to communicate with his or her fellow citizens. Music without a substantial audience is pointless. This is equally true of other areas of our cultural life.

As the sole purpose of the state is the well-being of its citizens, something which most governments seem to lose sight of, then that key element in this which we can term 'enrichment' becomes an obligation of the state. A government which thinks it can pull out of any cultural contribution is cheating on its citizens. Our Puritan traditions die hard and we find it easy to take up negative national obligations like defence, but positive enjoyments like culture are seen as something the citizen should fund him- or herself. The long and sterile debate over the financing of the BBC illustrates well this national frame of mind. It is generally agreed that the cultural contribution of broadcasting in Britain is exceptional by international standards. We have a system which delivers the goods. However, the fact that other countries favour commercial funding only of broadcasting tempts each British government, and particularly this one, to explore withdrawing the taxpayers' cash from the BBC. America is frequently quoted, despite having amongst the worst television and radio in the Western World. Only a fool would believe that the state's money is bad whilst private finance is always good. Since 1945 Britain has spent remarkably well its public money on cultural education. The one criticism is that there has been too little of it. The billions of pounds wasted on inept technical developments have no equivalent in terms of cultural investment.

Kenneth Lawson develops these themes and concludes 'culture and education seem to be irrevocably inter-related both to each other and to policies'. If we are to have a more self-confident population we may need to broaden the participation in the latter whilst ensuring more education. We should be showing some unease in a society where an hereditary crown prince can get professional changes in, say, architecture where the discontent of the citizenry apparently had less impact. This is all a trifle too feudal in a modern community with as rich a cultural tradition as anywhere in the world. As Marista Leishman states of one of the institutions here surveyed, 'the aim of the Trust is less to do with the implanting of knowledge than with the fostering of attitudes'. British popular attitudes too often range from indifference to apprehension when cultural matters are raised. As Edith Wharton wrote of a character, 'Mrs Ballinger is one of those ladies who pursue Culture in bands, as though it were dangerous to meet it alone'.

Britain has been evolving as a culture since the last Ice Age retreated, but never faster than during the last two hundred years of the Industrial Revolution. The latter, the môst all pervading development in human affairs since the Neolithic Revolution, began in Britain. Our culture has reflected such a uniquely pioneering role. It introduced a pace of change without parallel. This change continues unabated. It is not just that we have to accommodate remarkable technological developments, but also much more significant social ones. If, for example, we look at our cultural environment since 1945 we can see that we have only modest recognition by the state that we have become once more an obviously multicultural country. Substantial numbers of immigrants have settled from other major cultures. We might expect our dynamic native culture, which is a remarkable mix of borrowings to produce a distinctive Britishness, to move to the next stage of absorbing the cultures of these incomers to produce further richness. Our whole history has been one of endless immigrations to trigger new developments. Societies which remain lively and dynamic have as a crucial stimulus immigration. My Cornish forebears doubtlessly resented the arrival of the first wave of Celts, but they brought new ideas and ways as has every immigration since. We are a mongrel people and that has been our greatest strength. We have borrowed from everywhere to our huge social, economic and cultural benefit. In our modern environment we have available tools of considerable sophistication with which to promote cultural education, but we still rely on the will-power of the state to employ them. Other societies appear to have that will-power in a way we do not. Those who are familiar with, say, Australia will confirm this. A stimulating city like Melbourne is a glowing advertisement for the advantages of diversity of culture and enlightened government policies. By the twenty-first century Melbourne will have produced a new cultural mix which the rest of us will call 'Australian' without duly recognising its antecedents in Aboriginal Australia or Britain, or Yugoslavia, or Greece, or Vietnam, or Italy, or China. And yet it is the Inner London Education Authority which handles the largest number (172) of different languages spoken by those attending its schools in the world. London is an immigrants' city, as it has been throughout its history. The London-based Government might have been expected to be more interested in cultural education because of that fact, if not for a thousand equally important reasons.

A number of the contributors write of their provision in cultural education trying to, to use John Reeve's words, 'counteract stereotype and prejudice'. As with much of this first chapter this is a recognition that education brings greater enlightenment. We cannot afford to continue with our present under-educated population, and particularly in the area of cultural education. The world is getting much smaller. In 1870 the fastest tea-clipper would take 110 days to travel from Britain to Canton. Today I will complain of taking 19 hours to reach the much more distant Beijing in China. China is now on our doorstep, but our education system has done little to accommodate such dramatic changes.

Up to 1987 the Royal Air Force had 50 Jaguar aircraft crashes. The Jaguar costs something over £6 million which means that such losses had cost the British taxpayer £300 million. It is curious how we choose to spend our finite resources. As Kenneth Cooper states of the British Library, 'The Government's commitment to providing a new building at St Pancras is at once a powerful incentive and a strong guarantee for the role of the national library to be developed to meet the changing expectations and opportunities that lie ahead. That development will also depend on the adequacy of resources available for maintaining and preserving the collections, for exploiting information technology, for staffing the Library across the wide range of its activities. Clearly the overall level of resources available to the British Library is dependent, like so many other things, upon the level of prosperity of the nation. What is less well understood is that the converse is also true: the scale of annual financial support for the British Library will bear not only the effectiveness of the national library and information as a whole, but also on the future economic and cultural achievements of the United Kingdom.' All our political parties seem to see investment in cultural education as a drain on our resources whilst such activities are amongst the greatest sources of our prosperity. They weld together a diverse population, make it more stable and creative, give citizens a greater ability to function in a complex world, and earn billions of pounds directly from the results of cultural activities.

The following pages will illustrate these points well. Whether it is the contribution of the British Museum to the in-service training of teachers, or the Civic Trust's protection and improvement of the environment, or the Arts Council's attempts to define what is art, it will be seen that our society is permeated by the fall-out from our institutions of cultural education. What is central to such developments is the role of the state. If we have governments who claim to speak for our national values they must participate fully in our cultural education which promotes and extends such values. British governments often display an ambivalence in this area which must be derived from more substantial reasons than wishing to save money. These attitudes are more pertinent to the parliamentary debates of the early nineteenth century than to the late twentieth century when the state's role in promoting cultural education initiatives is much clearer. The cultural needs of the masses demand the resources of the masses, just as an aristocratic culture functioned on the resources of an interested gentry and its monarch. In the future the British government will find itself more deeply involved in the cultural education of its citizenry. This will obviously mean more state funding, but other areas will give Whitehall greater challenge. For example should the state provide cultural leadership or respond to the initiatives of others?

Chapter One

THE ARTS COUNCIL

David Jones

In this chapter I want to analyse the role of the Arts Council, as an agent of the State, in promoting cultural education in Britain. I will not solely be concerned with its role in promoting mainstream educational activity but also its role in setting the cultural and artistic agenda. I shall be concerned to examine the part the Council plays in establishing the cultural and artistic norms in our society and how, in so doing, influences the value system within which national artistic priorities are set. Additionally I am concerned to analyse the concepts of culture and cultural education as they relate to the work of the Arts Council. This is an area where there is often disagreement and where a polarisation of views sometimes occurs.

The chapter will focus mainly on adult education. When the term cultural education is used it is often seen as an aspect of permanent education, a concept which springs from and sits more easily in an adult education framework. Simpson sees permanent education as the way of bringing about that democratisation of culture which he seeks. He notes,

> Very briefly ... any system of education constructed in accordance with the principles of permanent education will enable people, throughout their lives, to have the means of self development, adaption to emerging needs and circumstances, and the full use of those resources, internal and external, which they possess for self-fulfilment ... Permanent education is, above all, education for change in a rapidly changing world; the concept of a once and for all initial education is

discarded in favour of a system which presupposes a life-long, though probably discontinuous recourse to education. (Simpson 1976:22-3)

Hence I make no apologies for viewing education as something which takes place throughout life and the compulsory sector as that part of education which, although the most financially aided, only caters for those between the ages of five and sixteen.

First, however, it is necessary to sketch in some background information about the Arts Council and its relationship to education. Following this I will offer an analysis of the nature of culture and of cultural education before going on to examine the Arts Council's contribution to cultural education.

THE ARTS COUNCIL AND EDUCATION

The Arts Council of Great Britain was granted a Royal Charter of Incorporation of 9th August 1946. The newly formed council was to continue the work of the Council for the Encouragement of Music and the Arts (CEMA) which had been set up following the outbreak of the Second World War in 1939. The Council was granted a new Charter in February 1967 under the terms of reference of which its objects were:

(a) To develop and improve the knowledge, understanding and practice of the arts;
(b) to increase the accessibility of the arts to the public throughout Great Britain;
(c) and to advise and co-operate with Departments of Government, local authorities and other bodies on any matters concerned whether directly or indirectly with the foregoing objects. (ACGB 1967)

From the granting of its first Charter until 1965 the Council received its moneys directly from the Treasury and was consequently responsible to the Chancellor of the Exchequer. From 1965, however, the grant was administered by the Department of Education and Science where a Minister of State was given special responsibility for the arts. This meant that the Secretary of State for Education and Science, after consultation with the Secretaries of State for Scotland and Wales, appointed the members and chairman of the Council. The vice chairman was appointed by the Council with the approval of the Secretary of State.

In 1985 the Council was granted a Supplemental Charter of Incorporation which gave it powers to administer the South Bank complex after the abolition of the Greater London Council. Under this Supplemental Charter the power to appoint the chairman and members to the Council was vested in the Chancellor of the Duchy of Lancaster. However, a type-written note enclosed with my copy of the Charter reads as follows,

From time to time ministerial functions referred to in the enclosed documents are transferred by Statutory Instrument to reflect government changes. Functions such as making appointments to the Arts Council of Great Britain are, in practice, undertaken by the Minister who has responsibility for the Arts. (ACGB 1985)

I think that it would be safe to assume that this gives a more accurate picture of the procedures than the precise wording of the charter.

Much of the way in which the Council sees its work and its relationship to education can be gleaned from its 'Memorandum to the House of Commons Select Committee on Education, Science and the Arts' (ACGB 1981). Here we are told that the Council sees its role as laying emphasis on co-operation between 'arts providers and education providers of all kinds'. Thus, over the years, both structurally through the DES and in policy terms it can be seen that the Council has acknowledged a liaison with the world of education. Just how this liaison has operated has depended on a variety of factors, not least the individual enthusiasms of Directors General and Chairmen of the Council. Indeed, from the early days, a link with education existed. Hutchison (1982:137) points out that,

W.E. Williams, Secretary of the British Institute of Adult Education, was one of the prime movers in CEMA, which was described in an early memorandum as concerned with 'activities on the fringe of adult education'.

In 1976 when (Sir) Roy Shaw, who had previously been a Professor of Adult Education, was Secretary General of the

Arts Council a number of events took place which set in train a movement that culminated in the eventual adoption of an educational policy by the Arts Council. I realise that it may be misleading to suggest that there were no moves towards the creation of an education policy before this date. I only wish to suggest that in 1976 there was a coincidence of events which helped to create a favourable climate of opinion. In this year the Council of Europe issued four publications which urged member Governments to take steps to involve greater numbers of their populations in the arts. Thus, Finn Jor (1976), Stephen Mennel (1976), Raymonde Moulin (1976) and J.A. Simpson (1976) added their voices to a growing movement for greater participation in the cultural and artistic life of the nation. Whilst these four books differed in their approach they were all to contribute to an upsurge in opinion about the need to take action to eradicate what some saw as the elitist image of the arts.

Another book was published in 1976 which, whilst not strictly concerned with education, did alert activists in this area to the fact that the funding agencies were not perhaps doing all they should to promote the arts of the whole population. This was Naseem Khan's book, The Arts Britain Ignores, The Arts of Ethnic Minorities in Britain. The book examined the art activities of Bangladeshis, Chinese, Cypriots, East and Central Europeans, Indians, Pakistanis, West Indians and the African contribution and concluded that they were, on the whole, excluded from mainstream arts funding. One of the main problems seemed to be that arts administrators, having been brought up and educated in a predominantly European tradition, were unable to make appropriate and necessary judgements about art forms from other and different cultural origins. The book recommended the funding of educational activity to raise consciousness about and expertise in art forms other than those springing from a white European base.

It is not claimed that any or all of these publications were directly instrumental in bringing about a new policy. All that is suggested is that they contributed to a tide of opinion on which the Arts Council's education policy was swept into place.

To add to this movement the Redcliffe-Maud report, Support for the Arts in England and Wales (1976), was published and educationalists everywhere, particularly adult educators, seized on the following quotation to support their case.

Within the next five years or so, the adult education movement must receive priority such as it has had at no time in our history, and when it does the arts must at last have their chance.

Meanwhile we must reject the long established fallacy that 'arts support' and 'education' are two separate things. More positively, we must insist that those responsible for them are natural allies, and see to it that they collaborate at national, regional and local levels. (Redcliffe-Maud 1976:23)

Taking this as its text a conference was organised in 1977 at Nottingham University under the joint auspices of The Arts Council of Great Britain, The National Institute of Adult Education, and the Calouste Gulbenkian Foundation to explore ways in which artists, arts providers and adult educators might work more closely together. This, together with pressure from the schools sector, contributed to a groundswell of opinion which led to the appointment, in 1978, of an Arts Council Education Liaison Officer funded by the Gulbenkian Foundation. This post was to become that of Senior Education Officer and become part of the Arts Council's permanent staff. An Assistant Education Officer was appointed later and eventually an Education Department established.

Two years after the Nottingham conference in 1977 the Arts Council arranged a recall conference to assess the development of the policies adopted in Nottingham. There were also many conferences at regional and local levels to find practical ways in which Adult Educators and Artists might be helped to collaborate. Many of these and subsequent developments are reviewed by Adkins (1981) in his book The Arts and Adult Education.

In 1981 the Arts Council issued a consultative document, The Arts Council and Education. The document invited responses from interested parties and after extensive consultation and the calling of a consultative conference led, in February 1983, to the formal adoption by the Council of an education policy (ACGB 1983). This movement towards the adoption of an educational policy was greatly assisted by the publication in 1982 of the Gulbenkian report, The Arts in Schools - Principles, practice and provision (Calouste Gulbenkian Foundation 1982). This document was itself influential in informing the practice of many of the Regional Arts Associations as well as that of educationalists.

By this time there was much collaboration taking place as a result of the consultations following the publication of the Redcliffe-Maud report. However the launch of the education policy was to generate a spate of interest in the Regional Arts Associations and add weight to the argument for the establishment of a small education budget to fund experimental and collaborative projects.

The role of education within the Arts Council was further strengthened in 1984 with the publication of their development strategy, The Glory of the Garden. The strategy generally sought to enhance the extent and quality of provision of the arts in the regions and on education stated,

> In order to encourage the continuation of education work, the Council will increase the money specifically allocated for this purpose. It has already announced that, in 1984/5, the sum available will be £160,000, almost double the sum available in 1983/4. For 1985/6, the sum will be almost doubled again to a total of £310,000. (ACGB 1984:20)

Thus, with the Arts Council giving the lead, the Regional Arts Associations and many of the Council's major clients began to take a more active interest in education and to seek ways of further collaborating with educational providers. The co-operation which the Redcliffe-Maud report had urged began to take place at 'national, regional and local levels'.

I recognise that this is a rather sketchy account of developments and that I have not detailed many of the factors which influenced the development of Arts Council policy in the field of education, not least the important contribution made by the education officers. My concern was to do no more than offer background information which will provide a framework and time-scale for the following discussion.

CULTURE AND CULTURAL EDUCATION

Any analysis of the ways in which the Arts Council contributes to cultural education in the United Kingdom depends very much on how one perceives the nature of culture and cultural education. There is a view which asserts that culture is what is sometimes described as 'high art', the sort of activity to which the Arts Council gives the greater proportion of its resources. Thus the literary, fine and the performed arts are thought to represent the highest expression of cultural achievement. In his report Support for the Arts in England and Wales Lord Redcliffe-Maud (1976:14) argued,

> By 'cultural' activities I mean all that involve any of the performing, visual, or literary arts and crafts mentioned above. Gardening, walking, riding, fishing and many other forms of sport and recreation are in some sense cultural activities but for my purpose I must concentrate on 'arts'.

Clearly the view here is one which sees 'cultural' activities as relating solely to traditional artistic activities. This interpretation stems from a tradition which dates back at least to the Renaissance; a tradition not without its detractors. In the same year as the Redcliffe-Maud report was published Simpson (1976:29), in his Council of Europe Publication, was arguing that such a view of culture was not as self-evident as might be supposed.

> Culture itself is no longer fully definable, or rather it has become blurred by a multitude of definitions ... Much of the difficulty has arisen by the importation, into the field of cultural policy, of the anthropologists' use of the word 'culture'. So used it means the behavioural norms and mores and values and attitudes and rules and taboos which make the framework of life in any given society.

He went on to argue that it was becoming increasingly difficult to defend 'the inegalitarian implications of a minority culture' whch was defined in terms of 'the tastes of a guiltily dominant class in a guiltily privileged area of the world'. Simpson (1976:34) finally settled for a pluralist definition of culture which was something far wider than the arts and humanities and which sprang not from an educated and sensitive elite but from the 'common man'.

Here we see illustrations of the two opinions which have occasionally polarised the debate on culture. There is

7

also evidence in Simpson's statement of the beginnings of a move to enlarge the interventionist role of supra-national agencies like the Council of Europe. Cultural exchanges of orchestras or national theatres were no longer felt to be enough. The development of cultural policy was to be placed in the hands of the people and reflect their diverse cultural aspirations. As will be explained later, this thinking was to have an important effect on the development of community arts organisations and the role of the regional arts associations.

It was recognised by some of those involved in this debate that the notion of what it means to be a cultured person is a social construct and not an unassailable fact of life. And if ideas of culture were socially constructed they could be challenged. Much writing from the community arts movement takes this line of argument. As Kelly (1984:88) points out,

> What had happened was that the interests of one group within society, that powerful group which ruled the Empire abroad and the factories and land at home, had come to set the standards of what it meant to be a cultured person. The tastes of this group were connected to what, in a previous era, had been the court arts; and they were located here for a variety of reasons, some of which were to do with education, and some of which were to do with aspirations of a newly ascendant group to legitimise itself socially.

There were others who were asking different but equally searching questions about the accepted concept of culture. In western industrialised countries culture was coming to be seen by some as a product of a capitalist consumer oriented society. Just as the Redcliffe-Maud report and Simpson's book were published Finn Jor added his voice. In his book, The Demystification of Culture (1976:29) he analyses the nature of 'elite' and 'popular' culture;

> We have already suggested that, broadly speaking, 'elite culture', as opposed to 'popular culture', is a historically and socially conditioned description. Thus, the struggle against the concept of an elite culture is in no small part an offshoot of the political struggle in this century. We must therefore go behind this frontier in order to find out what this culture really is, and what

the concept encompasses.

From time immemorial, cultural life has been thought of as a process, in which professionals (character-istically enough, 'creative artists') produce the cultural products, institutions and - in our time, the electronic media - disseminate them, while the public receives them. This pattern turns ordinary people into 'consumers' of culture, and important questions are left unanswered.

Clearly, there was a view, current amongst many in the arts world, that the arts were seen by funding bodies like the Arts Council as something to be provided, if not for the mass of the population, then for that proportion of the population which demonstrated an interest. But in the years since 1976 pressure to involve more people in the arts grew to the extent that the funding agencies were persuaded to devote increased resources to community arts and to education work.

There was a growing feeling amongst some commentators that art had been taken away from the people, that the state art industries were providing only for an elite minority and ignoring the vast majority of the population. They were doing this by defining art and culture in ways which excluded many more popular activities. Kelly analysed the situation thus:

> Art is an ideological construction; a generalisation which has a complex history through which its meaning has both shifted and narrowed. In its current usage its chief purpose is to bestow an apparently inherent value onto certain activities and the products resulting from these activities, while withholding this value from certain other similar activities. In this respect the term 'art' functions as one of a series of categories whose purpose is to assist in the construction and maintenance of a hierarchy of values which, having been constructed, can be made to appear as both natural and inevitable. (Kelly 1984:54)

For a time some artists and philosophers had been expressing concern that art was becoming divorced from its roots, that it was becoming the preserve of a small intellectual elite who could command vast sums of public money to subsidise their indulgence. The State it seemed was pouring resources into the maintenance of the pleasures of the few whilst ignoring the legitimate claims of the rest of society.

This argument was further fuelled by the fact that, whilst it was called the Arts Council of Great Britain, the largest proportion of the subsidy available went to London; in some years less than fifty per cent of the Council's spending was distributed throughout the rest of the country. A consequence of this is the perception that 'good art' occurs only in London and therefore ambitious artists gravitate towards the capital. Whilst there are arguments in favour of protecting national companies from the financial realities of the world of commerce, the fact that they were all perceived to be centred on the capital provided eloquent evidence for those who wished to argue against this centrist and unequal distribution of state funds. It is acknowledged that the Royal Shakespeare Company is, in fact, based at Stratford-upon-Avon but administratively and, to a certain extent philosophically, it seems to be based in the capital. English National Opera North is a fairly recent development and its establishment in Leeds was, in part, an attempt to counter-balance the domination of the metropolis.

There were other arguments in favour of bringing the arts back to the people. As long ago as 1968 Sir Herbert Read wrote a brief article expressing his worries about the growing trend towards internationalism in the arts. He was convinced, as had been many before him, that the creation of a work of art depended on a unique interaction between artist, materials and environment. He believed that art was related not only to the social and economic context in which it was created but more fundamentally to the very landscape of a country. He saw the international art industries as threatening this relationship. He was enough of a pragmatist to realise that he was not going to change the social order but nevertheless made this plea,

> If for economic and political reasons we must inevitably tend towards a worldwide social organization, and if this worldwide society is to be increasingly saturated with international periodicals, international exhibitions, the international exchange of artists and critics - a levelling out, that is to say, of artistic experience, can we, in such circumstances, preserve and cultivate the individual, the intimate, the regional and local grass-

roots of art? (Read 1968)

This view of the nature and source of art is not new. Historically art can be shown to be a societal activity which springs from rites, rituals and religious ceremonies of primitive tribal groupings. In such societies the distinction between what is and is not art become blurred. Art is both a mirror of and a way of understanding the world. Donald Horne explains the situation thus,

> In societies where participatory performing culture survived, such as that of the Australian Aborigines, the people, in dance and song, in instrumental music, drama and recitation, and in painting, themselves perpetuated the meaning they gave the world. The people themselves made their own 'art' (although to them there was no distinction between 'art' and the rest of their life). When they performed their festivals it was their equivalent of what we would now see as a multi-media presentation in a civic cultural centre - except that their presentation was not for an audience. In a modern industrial society our festivals are performed for us, usually on television screens. (Horne 1986:5)

There is a sense in which the arts become trapped by their own history. There seems to be a consensus that it is desirable to preserve examples of past art forms. Hence we have museums and art galleries and performances of drama and music from past and other cultures. Literature of the past is also studied and enjoyed. But what unfortunately seems to happen is that these art forms of the past become the dominant art forms. This is not to make any value judgements about their quality, but rather to suggest that the ever growing historical archive can be in danger of taking precedence over more contemporary and popular forms of cultural expression.

Thus the spectrum of opinions in the art world stretched from, on the one hand, those who saw art as a product, often created in an earlier age, to be consumed by the general public to, on the other hand, those who saw it as an activity in which to participate. The latter group felt that art had lost its roots and needed to redefine its role in terms which would bring about and draw strength from the involvement of greater numbers of people in creative activity. This view was attractive to teachers and gained

11

support from educators working across the spectrum of age groups. It was also taken up by many involved in the community arts movement.

On the other hand the 'art as consumer product view' saw art as the great historical legacy of European if not world culture. To this group the role of the state was concerned with the maintenance of high standards of performance and presentation and with ensuring the continued availability of opportunities to enjoy the arts, albeit as a consumer rather than as a participant.

Teachers, on the whole, sat uncomfortably in the middle of these two camps. Whilst they were usually in favour of participation by all in creative activity they could not put their hands on their hearts and argue against the maintenance of the cultural tradition. After all, they would all have had the benefit of higher education and with it that induction into the artistic standards and traditions which do so much to maintain the prevailing cultural norms.

There were, of course, good educational and developmental reasons for involving students in creative work. These had something to do with the benefits of self discovery through self expression and had their roots in developmental psychology. Such justifications of the work had nothing at all to do with challenging the prevailing cultural norms. Those supporting greater creative involvement in the arts, whilst sharing a common aim, often did so for different reasons; some saw it as a form of personal or community development whilst others were concerned politically to recapture the arts for the man in the street.

The two views are not, of course, irreconcilable and the Arts Council, like so many teachers, identified its role as pursuing both policy options at the same time. One can construct a continuum to demonstrate the range of opinion on this topic. On the one hand there are those who wish to preserve the great historical tradition in the arts. They wish to ensure that we can still listen to a Beethoven symphony or watch a performance of Oedipus Rex. They tend to see the artist as a special sort of person, gifted with a talent that the rest of us do not possess. The artist creates for the rest of us to enjoy (or 'consume', depending on one's point of view).

At the other end of the continuum are those who see art as part of a wider definition of culture. It is an activity which should relate to the whole of society and should spring from the localities and communities in which people live, work and celebrate. They believe that everyone has the ability to become involved in the creative process, either as an individual or in a communal activity. Art is something in which to participate. Adherers to this philosophy would reject the idea of art as a consumer product but would probably not go so far as to deny totally the desirability of an audience for some events.

The ways in which the Arts Council relates to this continuum are neither constant nor unified. Different sections of the Arts Council will see themselves as being at different points along the continuum. Over time the overall policy of the Council shifts in one direction or the other. Overall the Council seems to see its role as embracing the dual aims of maintaining opportunities to enjoy historical works whilst nurturing new developments in arts activity, no matter who or where they come from. Finn Jor noted this trend (1976:55).

But to an increasing extent, in country after country, it is being acknowledged that, just as the traditional cultural institutions should be maintained, society must also provide the less pretentious forms of culture with possibilities for self development.

The next section will examine ways in which the Arts Council attempts to do this.

THE ARTS COUNCIL AND CULTURAL EDUCATION

The Arts Council influences educational activity in a number of ways, some direct and some indirect. As mentioned earlier, perhaps the most important area of influence which the Council exercises rests in its contribution to deciding what will or will not be deemed to be art. Whilst being subject to the normal political pressures, from both government and activists in the field, the Arts Council retains a great deal of power and authority on artistic matters.

The so called 'arm's length principle' is described as a device for ensuring that there can be no party political governmental influence on the creative work of artists. The Arts Council is supposed to stand as a buffer between central government and the artist to ensure the maintenance of artistic freedom of expression. However, to assume that central government cannot or does not occasionally exercise control over the work of the Council would be a mistake. Appointing members of the Council is the prerogative of the government of the day and in so doing the party in power is bound to make a political choice. And occasionally one hears of politicians making life difficult for the Council by questioning particular artistic decisions.

It has to be said that until quite recently governments tried to adopt a bi-partisan approach to appointing members to the council; except, that is, for the appointment of the chairman who is usually seen to be a government sympathiser. This point was made recently by a former director general;

> ... arts policy has, until quite recently, continued to be bi-partisan, with the opposition party usually confining itself to criticising the ruling party for not giving enough subsidy. (Shaw 1987:30)

So far we have, in referring to the Arts Council, assumed that we were referring to the group of eighteen members, the chairman and vice chairman appointed by the Chancellor of the Duchy of Lancaster. But, of course, in the main the work of the Arts Council is carried out by its officers who also enjoy a great deal of discretion in what they choose to include in their concept of art. Whilst the seat of power is the Council itself, much of the authority is delegated to its full time officers. They, together with the Council's various advisory panels can be influential in setting the artistic agenda for the nation.

Additionally the Arts Council can exert an influence over the Regional Arts Associations. These bodies, twelve in all, are reponsible for the subsidy and promotion of artistic activity within a particular geographical area. They are usually governed by an executive committee which comprises representatives from the local authorities, artists and other interested parties in the region. They receive the main part of their grant from the Arts Council. In this respect they are responsible for implementing the Arts Council's policy throughout the country. Thus, the Arts Council can, through these bodies, influence the work being done in the regions. It was in this way that the Council was able to promote its educational policy.

It will be seen that through the Arts Council and the

Regional Arts Associations a structure exists which, to some extent, allows control over the level of subsidy if not the artistic content of arts activities throughout the nation. In this way, what is and is not to be considered as art can be subject to pressure from the centre. How and when this pressure is exercised varies from time to time. My concern here is not to point out how or why this power might be used or abused but to illustrate that the structures exist to facilitate its use.

The educational influence of the Arts Council is exercised through a number of channels. Clearly, the Council's Education Department plays a central role in deciding educational priorities for a given period of time and promoting these throughout the country. Additionally the Council can, through its advisory panels, bring pressure to bear on its clients to become more involved in educational activity. There is also an Education Bulletin which disseminates information about educational work in the arts. The Council can, on occasion, use its own resources to unlock funds from other agencies. Thus, an Arts Council grant may be used to persuade a Local Education Authority or charitable institution to offer a matching grant. In taking these sorts of initiatives the Arts Council can prioritise the activities it will fund in any given year and retain control of these priorities. These are some of the more obvious ways in which the Council influences education to bring about its objective of making the arts more accessible.

Since the adoption of its education policy the Arts Council has seen the main thrust of its education work in the promotion of joint ventures. From the point of view of adult education this term is defined by Adkins (1981:4) as follows:

> Joint ventures are schemes which bring people into contact with the professional arts or artists in organised learning situations arranged by arts providers and adult education providers. The working links between the providers, together with all the meetings, working parties, cross-memberships and so on, are examples of cooperation.

This definition can obviously be applied to all sectors of education. Adkins goes on to identify three main areas of joint-venture schemes as:

- appreciation courses addressed to the arts
- practical arts courses
- arts in the community (Adkins 1981:5)

These headings will serve as a framework for the following discussion of the Arts Council's educational activity.

Appreciation courses addressed to the arts have long been a feature of both the compulsory and non-compulsory sectors of education. Most children in school will spend some time reading works of literature, enjoying theatre and drama and learning about music, with perhaps some exposure to dance and an introduction to the visual arts and crafts. (Though these latter are more often tackled as a practical rather than a theoretical appreciative activity.) Adult education providers also include in their programme courses designed to help individuals to perceive better and thereby better enjoy a range of art forms. Additionally there are courses in the history of various art forms and whilst the focus here is obviously a historical one, they do contribute to the greater understanding and appreciation of the content and context of works of art.

If one were to try to categorise these courses in terms of the continuum of opinions on the nature of culture outlined in the previous section one would have to place them towards that view which saw art as objects for consumption and enjoyment, the 'high art' school of thought. In the main such courses deal with art that has already become respectable. Art is seen predominantly as part of a white western tradition. Increasingly, though, the arts funding agencies have acknowledged the arguments of those representing ethnic minority groups and have shown themselves willing to widen their concept of art to include much Afro-Caribbean and Asian work. However, much work still needs to be done in this area and, as Naseem Khan's book demonstrated in 1976, there was a great deal of ignorance, fear and prejudice which is only just beginning to be overcome.

The way in which the state, via the Arts Council and the Regional Arts Associations, becomes involved in such work is by sponsoring joint activity with an educational provider. Artists and craft specialists are placed in educational settings to work with teachers in bringing about a greater understanding of both their own and others' creative work. Additionally resident and touring theatre, opera and ballet companies, along with major orchestras, are being encouraged by the Arts Council to involve themselves in educational activity such as pre- or post-performance lectures, visits to schools and colleges and workshops for teachers and pupils. This list is not intended to be comprehensive. It simply illustrates some of the ways in which the Arts Council becomes involved in helping individuals to appreciate the arts.

Like appreciation courses, practical art courses have always had their place in the curriculum, across the whole spectrum of educational provision. As hinted at earlier, creative work was thought by psychologists from Jung onwards to contribute to the development of the personality and to lead to a greater degree of self awareness. This gave it an important role in the area of child education. Increasingly, however, personal development is becoming seen to be a life-long process and it is accepted that individuals continue to develop and mature throughout life. The years of compulsory schooling are only a small part of this process; less and less are these years being seen as some sort of preparation which will equip individuals for the rest of their days. Consequently, the value of creative work for adult development is being re-assessed. Just as education is being increasingly seen as a life-long process, so creative art courses are increasingly being seen as contributing to the maintenance and integrity of the adult psyche.

In terms of our continuum of opinion these courses tend towards that end which sees art as a participatory activity, accepts the creative potential of all and wishes to bring art back to its roots in the community. Though, it has to be said, exposure to the arts in this sort of way can, and often does, lead to an interest in the arts generally, an interest in specific art forms, artists or historical periods and styles, and a desire to explore the artistic traditions now represented in our ethnically and culturally diverse society.

As with appreciation courses, the Arts Council encourages its clients to become involved with educational providers in mounting practical courses designed to foster creative activity. Again specialists from the arts and crafts, from the worlds of drama, literature and music are invited to run workshops, master classes, creative writing courses and to participate in multi-media creative activity with non-specialist children and adults.

At this point it is interesting to focus on the performed arts. In this area, educational activity seems to be biased

17

towards the development of the skills of the performer rather than the creator. There are any number of courses for the instrumental player, the actor or the dancer but few for the composer, the dramatist or the choreographer. This may simply be a question of scale; there is more demand for actors, instrumentalists and dancers than there is for playwrights, composers and choreographers. But it may also be symptomatic of a more fundamental misunderstanding, a misunderstanding about the nature of creative activity. The concepts of creating and performing often get mixed up and both teachers and artists are sometimes given to believing that they are creating when in fact they are performing. There is a sense in which the performing artist is the tool of the creative artist. The performer is part of the medium in which the creative artist is working. In educational terms it is desirable to develop both creative and performing skills. There is a danger in believing that we are doing the former when we are doing the latter.

At the extreme end of the continuum are those creative activities which go no further than their immediate situation. They are for and by an individual or a group and they are not seen as being aimed at the production of an artefact. Their purpose is to do with the expression of a community identity in celebration or in protest. They may celebrate or deprecate either the past, present or future. They are those sorts of activities which characterise much community arts work.

Community Arts is not a term which represents a particular art form but rather an attitude or relationship to the arts. The community arts movement sprang from the great upsurge in experimental art forms during the sixties. The various arts labs, arts centres, and the experiments at Stratford East and with Centre 42, a trade union backed drama enterprise, contributed to the working out of an approach to the arts which involved ordinary people in arts activities. Community arts is partly a political movement which seeks to ensure that local communities can take charge of their own artistic activity. It is concerned to redefine culture and art in terms which would have appealed to Jor and Simpson and which reflects their thinking as set out in the Council of Europe publications of 1976.

Community Arts has much in common with radical adult education. It is concerned with empowerment, with enabling members of the community to take control of their own artistic development and to develop their own unique cultural and artistic identity.

The processes by which the community arts movement achieves its aims are similar to and probably derived from much community development work. Ideally the community artist should be responsive; the initiative to inaugurate some sort of project should come from the community itself. The community artist then provides expertise, help and advice but ensures that control of the creative process remains with the community. It will be seen that this is very different from that sort of 'artist in the community' scheme whereby an artist is given facilities to continue with his or her own work in a situation which is thought to be more accessible to the general public, thus bringing about greater dialogue between artist and community. Such schemes may do much to demystify the arts and to spread knowledge about the nature of the arts and artists. However, they do little to redefine the nature of culture or the control of creative activity. The community artist, on the other hand, wishes to bring about the creative development of individuals in a spirit of communal activity.

This is the ideal. What has often happened, however, is that a Regional Arts Association has appointed an animateur or an artist in residence to try to activate a community. The artist may have been attached to a school or community centre and their job was to set up some sort of support group which would serve as a nucleus for the formation of a community arts project. This group would decide upon the nature of artistic activity in which it wanted to become involved and devise ways of including more members of the local community. The community artist would, initially, act as a resource with the ultimate intention of handing over complete control to the community arts group.

Many groups, however, quite liked the idea of having a full-time organiser at their disposal and were unwilling to give up the resources invested in this person. Consequently there are now projects which, though controlled by members of the community, depend on the work of one or more full-time paid officials. Other projects use resources in a different way. Rather than investing in full time workers they hire, on either a part-time or a temporary basis, the expertise they need for a particular project. Thus, they may hire a dramatist or theatre specialist to help them with the development of some documentary drama or a painter to help with a mural.

Other schemes reflect both these trends by having a

full-time worker and hiring part-time help as and when necessary. Yet other schemes are run on an entirely voluntary basis. Su Braden in Artists and People provides an analysis of some of the ways in which artists relate to communities but Kelly (1984) provides a more up to date critique. There is still a need for a thorough analytical evaluation of community arts work.

All this work is funded largely by the Regional Arts Associations. This represents one of the key ways in which an arm of the state becomes involved in cultural education; involved in activity, the very purpose of which, is to open up the culture business to both the community and to creative development. It is a way in which the RAAs can loosen the bonds which have constrained our concept of the arts for so long.

There are, as one might expect, grave worries about how such community arts work might be evaluated. The arts funding agencies are used to basing their evaluations on an aesthetic appraisal of a work of art or of a performance. This is all very straightforward. There is, they believe, general agreement about what constitutes a 'good' work or performance and they can apply well tried criteria. And, after all, since they, the funding agencies, are setting the agenda they must clearly embody the expertise to evaluate it. When, however, the agenda is set elsewhere, and is different from that of the experts in the Regional Arts Associations and when, moreover, that agenda includes criteria which are not solely aesthetic ones but are both educational and developmental, then the extent of the threat felt by some arts administrators can be appreciated.

Community Arts is riddled with such difficulties and contradictions. When the Arts Council devolved responsibility for Community Arts to the Regional Arts Associations it was said by some that this was because the Council, which, after all, represents the national repository of expertise in the arts, could not handle such a controversial issue. Whether or not this assertion is true is open to question for, after all, it does make sense to site control of a community activity at a local rather than a national level. Nevertheless the difficulties in relation to evaluative criteria should not be underestimated.

Many attempts to popularise creative activity in the arts have aroused fears about the maintenance of standards. These are not only levelled at activists in the community arts movement but at other sectors of education. Boris Ford

(1980) at a conference organised jointly by the Arts Council and New Universities Quarterly bemoaned the state of education in the arts as follows,

> Thus one has seen in the past generation the cult of the avant-avant-garde in arts colleges at the expense of an apprenticeship in draughtsmanship and design. The music academies, on the other hand, maintain their preoccupation with technical virtuosity at the expense of an education in musical standards and renewal. As for the creative writer - he remains uninstructed, at best self instructed: while the departments of literature, which for many years have gone in for variants of literature criticism, now teeter on the brink of continental philosophies which reject the autonomy of the reader, the authority of the author and the clear-cut meaning of the text.

The world of the professional artist and the world of education often enter periods where they live very uneasily together; periods when the basic philosophies of both education and the arts are challenged and reassessed. Since 1976 there has been a remarkable period of mutual respect, understanding and joint activity. In this chapter I have attempted to identify the historical forces which brought this about. It is difficult to say where this movement will lead. The conceptual framework within which artists and educators operate is still being questioned and argued through. One hopes that such a reappraisal will lead to a cultural plurality which values equally the many artistic traditions represented in Britain and at the same time allows activity on a local community level. One could do no better perhaps than to echo Donald Horne.

> If we were to make a declaration of cultural rights, what rights would we declare? It is possible to imagine them in three interconnected groups: rights of access to the human cultural heritage; rights to new art; rights to community art participation. (Horne 1986:234)

This declaration could well point the way for the Arts Council's continued involvement in cultural education.

BIBLIOGRAPHY

ACGB, 1967, The Charter of Incorporation granted by Her Majesty the Queen to The Arts Council of Great Britain, London, Arts Council of Great Britain

ACGB, 1981, Memorandum Submitted by the Arts Council of Great Britain to the House of Commons Select Committee on Education, Science, and the Arts, London, Arts Council of Great Britain

ACGB, 1981, The Arts Council and Education, London, Arts Council of Great Britain

ACGB, 1983, The Arts Council and Education, A Policy Statement, London, Arts Council of Great Britain

ACGB, 1984, The Glory of the Garden. The Development of the Arts in England, London, Arts Council of Great Britain

ACGB, 1985, The Supplemental Charter of Incorporation granted by Her Majesty the Queen to The Arts Council of Great Britain, London, Arts Council of Great Britain

Adkins, G., 1981, The Arts and Adult Education, Leicester, ACACE

Calouste Gulbenkian Foundation, 1982, The Arts in Schools - Principles, practice and provision, London, Calouste Gulbenkian Foundation

Braden, S., 1978, Artists and People, London, Routledge and Kegan Paul

Ford, B., 1980, 'Excellence and Standards in the Arts', in New Universities Quarterly, Volume 35, No. 1, Winter 1980/81, Oxford, Basil Blackwell

Horne, D., 1986, The Public Culture - The Triumph of Industrialism, London, Sydney etc., Pluto Press

Hutchison, R., 1982, The Politics of the Arts Council, London, Sinclaire Browne

Jor, F., 1976, The Demystification of Culture: Animation and Creativity, Strasbourg, Council of Europe

Kelly, O., 1984, Community Art and the State: Storming the Citadels, London, Comedia Publishing Group

Khan, N., 1976, The Arts Britain Ignores, The Arts of Ethnic Minorities in Britain, London, Community Relations Commission

Mennel, S., 1976, Cultural policy in Towns, Strasbourg, Council of Europe

Moulin, R., 1976, Public Aid for Creation in the Plastic Arts, Strasbourg, Council of Europe

Read, H., 1968, 'The problem of Internationalism in Art',

The Magazine, Oct. 1968, London, The Institute of Contemporary Arts

Redcliffe-Maud, Lord, 1976, Support for the Arts in England and Wales, London, Calouste Gulbenkian Foundation

Shaw, R., 1987, The Arts and the People, London, Jonathan Cape

Simpson, J.A., 1976, Towards Cultural Democracy, Strasbourg, Council of Europe

Chapter Two

THE BRITISH COUNCIL

Paul Fordham with Warren Shaw

> 'The British Council's purpose is to project Britain abroad' Council Publicity leaflet 1986 (The British Council Promoting Britain Abroad).
> 'The purpose of the British Council is to improve international understanding'. Council publicity leaflet 1986 (Using Britain).

The spate of recent literature about the British Council is in danger of turning into a flood. We have a detailed official history of the first fifty years (Donaldson 1984), an analysis of its role in international cultural relations (Mitchell 1986) and, above all, the several government reports (notably Duncan 1969, Central Policy Review Staff 1977 and Seebohm 1981) and the six internal Activity Reviews which have examined and re-examined the public policy issues. As a result some things have changed.

The Council now sees itself as more cost effective: certainly direct government grant has been cut by 20 per cent since 1980 and yet over-all activities have increased partly by means of greatly expanded direct earnings. Public relations have greatly improved. More positively, there seems general agreement that the Council's business is with cultural relations rather than cultural diplomacy and that short term political or commercial advantage is less its business than longer term and widespread understanding of British values, the English language and British culture broadly defined. The Council is still, in fact, a largely educational institution rather than the 'UK Ltd.' some cynics have dubbed it: the Representative abroad still an independent professional of integrity, rather than a mere cultural attaché.

And yet the Council has never been studied as a great educational institution. There are ambiguities in its own view of itself which can lead to uncertainty or muddle, so that a sensitive and sympathetic observer can still comment that a 'tradition of good service it has certainly established; a well-nourished and secure sense of an intellectual tradition germane to its own purposes it has not; it has been jolted too often' (Hoggart 1986:7).

The rest of this chapter offers some reflections on the Council as educational institution in relation to: context; programmes; the exchange of people; the principle of mutuality; the place of culture in development (including relations with ODA); promoting Britain and increasing 'international understanding'.

CONTEXT

Mitchell (1986-87) points out that there are three established models for the conduct of cultural relations with varying degrees of government control and influence. France operates a system of firm government control, Germany a mixed system of government and voluntary agencies, while Canada and the UK entrust their cultural relations to non-governmental autonomous agencies. This is not generally recognised, especially in Britain itself. The British Council is often assumed by people outside it to be a direct arm of Government. But its autonomy is an important guarantee of separation from the day to day conduct of diplomacy and hence an ability to be concerned with long term rather than short term aims.

There are clear parallels with the Arts Council or the BBC in organisation; but whereas the former operates in a purely national context, the British Council (like the BBC World Service) has constantly to determine what, how and to whom it shall project a British perspective. It is Britain abroad, not Britain at home, and the evident lack of any clear intellectual tradition 'germane to its purpose', may here seem to put it at some disadvantage with the much clearer political directives of, say, an east European cultural mission or the confident mission civilisatrice of the French. At the time of the Council's establishment in the 1930s:

Any notion that Britain had a sacred duty to spread its
culture (as distinct from its order or its justice) would
have found favour with few of its subjects. For one
thing, culture was not a concept that attracted
enthusiasm within Britain: the compound parts of
culture - literature, language, the arts, architecture,
horticulture, sport - all had their exponents and
advocates, but Britain did not, like France, possess the
intellectual tradition of seeing them collectively as an
expression of nationhood and certainly not as something
that should be transmitted to others. (Mitchell 1986:35)

The stark contrasts in French and British colonial policy
during the twentieth century illustrate the quite different
attitudes to cultural relations. The French in Africa created
an élite group who were culturally French in all but
geographical location and, for those who looked to
'negritude', perhaps pigmentation. But the British neither
wished nor thought it possible to do any such thing. They
kept themselves to themselves and, wherever possible, they
chose to rule indirectly through 'native' authorities, as in
northern Nigeria or the Indian princely states. Partly by
default there was thus greater respect for local languages
and culture and, even where British settlers dominated, the
school system ensured that local cultural growth was not
entirely stifled. Linguistic pluralism may have impeded the
growth of a coherent educational system, but at least there
were some cultural roots left to nurture.

In former French West Africa the visitor to Abidjan
today can be forgiven for wondering whether this is really
west Africa or a Paris suburb transported to a tropical sea
shore. Poodles in the park, an excellent public transport
system, metered taxis, Evian water in the Monoprix ... On
the other side of the continent in former British East
Africa, Nairobi seems more an amalgam of influences. A
powerful Indian contribution, confident Africans adopting
(and adapting) selectively from British culture: an
incomplete synthesis of cultures rather than total immersion
in one. And yet this contrasting picture may itself be a
typically British illusion. Twenty years on I still remember
the surprise I felt myself at the culture shock experienced
by a young visiting lecturer (American) to Kenya. What
really got under his skin was that it was all 'so damned
British'. He felt much more threatened by that than
anything he yet perceived in local (African) ways of doing

things.
The important contextual point is this. The idea of 'British culture' is itself alien to British culture. We are too philistine, too anti-intellectual in our style to want to have that kind of clear intellectual tradition for our institutions or for others to follow. And yet the English language, the ideas it embodies and the ways of living it evokes are all powerful and continuing influences. We do not have to be self-consciously cultural to promote British culture. It is the very absence of any secure intellectual tradition which now becomes a strength in the post-imperial world. We can promote British interests while seeming to be modest, even self-deprecating. We can be sensitive to what is locally valued and know how to be equally sensitive about the 'curriculum' we choose to promote. The absence of an intellectual imperative gives the Council the freedom to be flexible and is an encouragement to practice mutuality in cultural education and interchange. This puts enormous responsibility onto the shoulders of individual Representatives. There is freedom to fail as well as to succeed, and the ways of promoting Britain or increasing understanding will vary quite markedly not only because Thailand is not Tanzania, but because of the many different day to day decisions of locally based staff.

PROGRAMMES

'Whether by design or default the Council is increasingly becoming the agent of other people's bidding.' This is the conclusion of the Director General in his Report for 1986-87. It derives from the fact that whereas total programmes have continued to increase both in volume and in costs the balance of funding has shifted towards direct earnings (over 22%) and directly funded Government programmes (over 48%). The money which can be spent by the Council as free agent (i.e. the Council's government grant) is now less than thirty per cent of the total budget; it amounts to some £75m or more than £20m less in real terms than in 1978-79. In that year the principal Government grant was 46% of total budget.
. Thus the freedom to be flexible referred to earlier is in fact very severely constrained. The work of individual Representatives can easily be dominated by the demands of the market or of the overwhelming size of the ODA

sponsored aid programme. In 1986-87 there were five countries where the Council had a budget of over £8m: India (£17.5m), China (£11.5m), Kenya (£8.6m), Nigeria (£8.5m) and Spain (£8.2m). The first four are dominated by the aid programme (e.g. in the case of Kenya 90% of expenditure) while Spain, with extensive English language teaching, is the best money earner for the Council in western Europe (88% of the country budget).

The largest identifiable money earner is English language teaching. This is not only a perceived market success but does, of course, fit in with the Council's central mission of cultural education and with those parts of the aid programme (especially in Commonwealth countries) concerned to preserve and enhance the status and use of the English language. If the Council can be said to have a core curriculum the label would have to be applied to English language teaching.

And yet the very success of this core activity points up the dangers of having to follow a purely commercial demand or the instrumental view of language teaching which political policy makers seem to see as necessary. As Hoggart argues, language is not just a technology.

> To make it purely 'instrumental' is to damage that language's access to its tap roots. It will survive, but, in the end, in a denatured form. (1986:126)

When literature was placed with English Language Division in 1981 it was hoped that the tap roots would thereby be fed. This seems not to have happened, no doubt because of the overwhelming size of the language operation. Nevertheless, it seems something of a gesture of despair that Hoggart should now recommend the safety of the Arts fold for literature rather than a greater determination (including more resources) to achieve better cross fertilisation (1986:136). Is the Council's language teaching to remain forever entirely instrumental?

For the rest the Council's programmes are concerned with a very wide range of information services, libraries, the promotion of British science and the arts - and with exchanging people. To many Representatives the library remains the core of all the promotional programmes. It is the long term visible and greatly used presence when visiting artists have departed or consultants gone their transient ways. It can even be the library for an expanding small town, as I first learned when organising adult education classes in Kenya in the 1960s. Twenty years later the Council's library in Kisumu still maintained its welcoming presence: visibly British but also visibly a major educational resource for that rapidly growing town. When I visited Argentina in 1985 and had the opportunity to talk informally to Argentinians at an international conference, we expressed mutual regrets at the continuing lack of 'relations'. But, they complained, if we could not even get started on Las Malvinas, could we not at least re-open the British library? All that unused educational resource ...

THE EXCHANGE OF PEOPLE

It is here - and with the related issue of mutuality, that there is greatest sensitivity - and opportunity - both for the promotion of Britain abroad and for an increase in international understanding. But particularly in the Council's relations with developing countries there is an inevitable unevenness: students coming to Britain, teachers going to developing countries. In each case the flow of ideas seems largely from the teacher (British) to the taught (foreign). Ali Mazrui has recently commented about this unevenness and about the dangers of 'cultural dependence rather than cultural interdependence' (Mazrui 1986:5).

> Whatever should be done? The bringing in of teachers from the Third World to teach in British colleges would be a significant improvement over just bringing in students. The presence of foreign students in Britain does enrich the population to some extent, but it remains true that the degree to which they become Anglicized is greater than any cultural relevance they might have to the British way of life.

In 1986-87 there were more than 26,000 people visiting Britain under Council auspices, most of them students. They Came to Train (Williams 1985) is the most thorough study of the impact of the British experience; and they did indeed come to 'train' in a very wide range of disciplines and skills. But what of the impact of British values and way of life? Is this an effective and mutually rewarding experience of cultural education? Some answers - albeit tentative - emerge from a research study conducted for ODA in 1982-

29

83. This was an evaluative study of post-graduate adult education courses at five UK universities. Two major issues of cultural importance seemed significant for these students; the first curricula and the second their experience of living in Britain (Fox et al. 1987).

The curriculum issues are inevitably too particular and too detailed to be dealt with fully here. But the outstanding issue - relevance to 'back home' professional tasks - is of general importance. Most students come to Britain to secure a qualification. Theirs are highly instrumental concerns and, inevitably, the cultural impact desired by their sponsors must be incidental rather than direct. And yet there is evidence that the content of some courses has greater value from the students' point of view where the material is obviously less culture bound. They showed some suspicion of content which seemed too UK orientated and were much happier with, say, comparative studies. Above all they valued familiarity with fundamental theory or ideas which have universal rather than particular validity. Nevertheless, the same study shows that for many respondents an important benefit of residence in Britain was the experience of interaction with another culture; and opportunity to explore new territory, to acquire new perspectives. On the other hand, the evidence shows that for many it was sometimes a lonely experience in Britain - often simply membership of a small group of fellow countrymen isolated from the communities in which they were living. Such evidence was echoed more recently in a private conversation (1984) with a Malaysian MP who 'blamed' the UK for encouraging religious fundamentalism in his country because students were isolated within the student communities.

The problem of 'social isolation' was identified by tutors as well as students, although its origins are not to be found only in the 'alien' culture which students find themselves in.

Many people coming here do, perhaps, see their role in rather narrow terms. They see themselves as coming to study and acquire a qualification at the end of it. Now I would be really happy if people also came here thinking what a marvellous opportunity it is to be in a foreign country and to get to know something about the culture. They have spent their time in their own hostel room or in the library or possibly with one or two of their own compatriots or othe overseas students, living very isolated lives, when in fact there is an enormously interesting culture and history waiting to be discovered. (Brian Hughes, Southampton)

Some argued pressure of work:

Doing a PhD is very demanding. You spend most of your time at your desk and in the library. (Kenyan - Hull - 1983)

Some claimed that too few events - or not the right ones - were organised for them:

We felt cut off. There was nobody to take us around. The British Council was playing a very paternalistic role, because, other than very official very formal conducted tours, they didn't encourage interaction outside the classroom. People ended up in small groups. If there wasn't another Kenyan I would have looked for another fellow from Africa to have someone to talk to. (Kenyan - Hull 1979) (Fox et al. 1987:113)

For others it was the stipend or the 'reserve' of the British - although it does seem that the further north in Britain you travel, though the weather gets colder, the emotional climate is warmer!

Despite the occasional criticisms of the formality of the receptions or other events, there were many appreciative remarks about the work of the British Council local offices where they are established:

The British Council local office in Hull was extremely useful, and I was very sorry when I came to hear that they have closed down. Those were the people who seemed to have a lot of experience of overseas students. I visited the office regularly - every week three or four times - and we found that whenever we had any problems there were people ready to help us. (Kenyan - Hull - 1979 in Fox et al. 1987:117)

In this respect those students who came under the auspices of the Council were much more fortunate than those who were not supported by an agency. And it is sad to have to record that since this study was undertaken there has been a rationalisation of UK based services and the pruning of local offices; this is regretted by all those who are concerned about the welfare of overseas students.

For those students, however, who had regularly attended church there was a much greater opportunity to be more in touch with the local community. In the diaries and in the interview conversations there are many accounts of visiting local homes, giving talks about life in Africa and the forming of friendships.

The attitude of the teaching staff was singled out as a very important factor in creating the sense of being welcome and in counteracting the possibilities of isolation. Some students reported relationships both in and outside the classroom as being fluid and reciprocal;

> We got a chance to discuss together, to ask questions and feel free with that. Also, on the social side, the lecturers treated us like friends or as part of the staff. (Tanzanian - Southampton - 1983)

> It wasn't like a student relationship. There was a sharing of ideas together. They respected our views and they also wanted to learn from us. (Ghanaian - Southampton - 1983)

Others, however, reported a mixed reaction to the way the staff related to the students. On the one hand are comments of the order that some of the staff 'treated us as people with useful knowledge to contribute'. On the other hand others 'tried to teach us like students'.

It was a student from Manchester who said that within a minute or so you could tell whether a tutor had experience of Africa. It seems to have made a great difference not only to the content of the programme, but also the quality of the relationship:

> There were those who treated us as students and those who really made you feel that you were

more than a student, who encouraged a freedom of communication. Those who had had experience outside the UK were better at communicating with us than the others. They knew how senior we were: they had some respect. (Kenyan - Manchester - 1978) (Fox et al. 1987:118)

Studying abroad is bound to involve times of isolation and loneliness. And it is clear that this can best be minimised and cultural interchange enhanced if there are positive efforts to do so. Organisations (like local British Council offices) can be very important in this cultural interchange. Above all, it is likely to be the efforts of countless individuals who believe in and promote reciprocal relationships.

THE PRINCIPLE OF MUTUALITY

The principle of mutuality lies at the heart of the successful exchange of people; it is also a central part of the possible conflict of interest expressed in the quotations at the head of this chapter. If 'promotion' is the sole aim, then mutual 'international understanding', either bilateral or multi-lateral, can only arise through similar (and equal) promotional activities by other countries. This would be to see the Council as a free market export agency with culture as its product and all parts of the world as exploitive potential. But education through knowledge and understanding - the long term process of developing cultural relations which are sensitive to a range of other cultures - can only be achieved if the starting point is a belief in mutual benefit.

We have seen that the Representative in any given country can only make real choices - whom to contact, how, when and for what purposes - with the free money (i.e. government grant) available in that particular place; this may be as little as 10% of the total budget. Nevertheless it is what enables each office abroad to develop its own distinctive style, its own 'curriculum' and its own sense of what aspects of a rich and complex culture are appropriate to that time and place. In undertaking this task the Representative has to act like an adult education organiser. Local wants are often made manifest: more scholarships, financial support, a library, Landrovers. But how to translate these into needs which themselves meet the aims and objectives of the Council? No outsiders can begin to do this unless they have a sensitive understanding of what is important locally and what may be seen to have potential. Mutuality is not merely an arguable ideological position: it is the sine qua non for effective working. More stress on the principle of mutuality was a major recommendation of the Hoggart report (1986:69-70) while Williams (1986:80-4) has derived a 'mutuality table' which assesses both promotion ('a scale of projection from the modest desire to achieve recognition to the more assertive desire to indoctrinate') and receptivity to the cultural scene in the host country. All the five Representatives interviewed for the purpose of this chapter stressed the importance of this principle.

An exchange of people with mutual interests may be more difficult, but it is certainly of more long term benefit to British cultural education than the usual teachers-out-students-in pattern. And an imported chamber music concert which appeals only to a small group of local expatriates is certainly of less significance than, say, a visiting theatre group which works with local teachers in developing drama in education. Long term 'links', as for example those between university departments are likely to be more enriching than one off contacts.

There is a case for occasionally promoting the best of British culture. The example of the London Symphony Orchestra playing in Bangkok was quoted to me in interview. Over 3,500 people came but the time and energy of the staff were mightily stretched in its promotion. However, in a less confident local culture such an exotic import might have been a total flop. Again, like any good adult education organiser, the Representative has to be sensitive to what is possible rather than just what may seem desirable.

Perhaps the overwhelming concern in promoting culture in a reciprocal way is to avoid being either dominating or patronising. As Ali Mazrui points out (1986:5):

It is of course possible to promote British interests without attempting to impose any sort of hegemony ... very often people involved in cultural diplomacy form a 'reverse lobby' and tend to defend the overseas constituencies in which they operate ... So cultural diplomats in the Third World often serve more than one function: they are in the first instance apologists for their own cultures and in the second instance they become this counter lobby, helping their bases understand the societies in which they operate.

The importance of sustained contact between two active partners cannot be overestimated and, again, the role of an effective Representative is crucial. What happened to the 'Culturas' (Anglophil Institutes) in Latin America in the 1950s is an object lesson for today's policy makers. In 1951-52 there were 6,000 students using the Cultura in Buenos Aires (still the home of the closed British library mentioned earlier), 4,000 in Rio de Janeiro, 4,000 in Rosario, 2,600 in Montevideo, 3,000 in Mexico City and 1,800 in Lima (British Council Annual Report 1952). By any standards a useful volume of activity.

However, the Culturas were cast off by the Council as economies during massive cuts of the 'fifties, and became more and more identified with the interest of local Anglophils, typically aristocratic and élitist Latin Americans including some of British stock, or long-term resident British businessmen. They are predominantly Anglophil within the terms of the target country's Anglophilia (which usually means as defined by the 'Anglo-community' of that country). The interests and policies of the British Council - or of the British government - do not necessarily coincide with these.

In the absence of effective Council representation it would be surprising if mutuality survived in other than a distorted form. Privatisation is not a new phenomenon; but this Latin American example might give pause to those who contemplate more of it or who see an even greater emphasis in future for purely market forces.

THE PLACE OF CULTURE IN DEVELOPMENT

Too often development is seen purely in economic terms. As more than one Representative complained to me in conversation, aid policy (determined by the Overseas Development Administration) is economic development led and pays scant regard to cultural matters. Perhaps this is a continuing reflection of British embarrassment at promoting matters cultural, or perhaps just a reflection of the market philosophy of our time. Hoggart (1986:37) recommended discussions between the Council and ODA towards 'a more flexible definition of development', not least because cultural development is seen by developing countries themselves as an important part of the search for national identity and unity. However, it is not merely a very important dimension it is also the most difficult and the most sensitive. It is here that the maintenance of mutuality presents the most challenging task for any Representative.

The cultural dimension for aid giving countries consists in mediating between their own culture and values and those of developing countries. Inevitably there will be a flow of influences from a dominant to a receptive society; this has happened in all periods of history. The task of cultural agencies is to make this process beneficient and to modulate its effects ... (Mitchell 1986:90)

Mitchell suggests that, in developing countries especially, a cultural agency can too easily adopt superior, dismissive attitudes and establish contact with ready-made local minority groups that echo the attitude of insensitivity to local culture. That there are many examples of this does not make a general rule: in more and more developing countries the emergence of radical politics militates against such patronising attitudes. It is the function of the cultural agency to find empathy with the new nation and an understanding of its aims and where they have mutual contact. For example, one of the most feared radicals in the new Ghana government of 1982 proved to have been a frequent reader in the British Council's library: while he opposed current western and British politics he shared its intellectual heritage. Once this was understood, new approaches could be made to bridge the gap made by immediate political difficulties between the new government and British educational and training aid offers.
The Mitchell principle was not necessarily true in the Council's early colonial days, heavy with the influence of expatriates. There was the occasion in pre-independence Tanganyika when, for immediate political reasons, the British Council Representative found himself forbidden to contact government teachers going to Britain on courses, but he was able to continue to act as a go-between for the Council with mission or privately funded teachers through a sympathetic returned teacher: the future President Julius Nyerere.

In its development of contact in ex-British colonies, the Council has gone through several stages. First, the 'Colonial' (nineteen-forties to early 'sixties): where the Council was typically a library with a club atmosphere, holding debates, running amateur dramatics or perhaps a hockey team; giving knife and fork drill for those privileged to go on scholarships to Britain, but without its own entry to schools, since education was a Colonial Office-financed operation and no two UK-financed operations could be allowed to spend money on the same object. Many leading African novelists and librarians started their careers in these centres.

The second stage came in the 'sixties of early independence with the Council's entry into education, perhaps with an English Language Officer or a Science Education Officer who could offer in-service training opportunities. With the Ashby Report came technical assistance funding for large-scale in-country training courses (known at first as 'Ashby Courses' then becoming institutionalised as 'Teacher Vacation Courses' until they became such an annual budgetary ritual that the ODA felt obliged to move their funding to other operations). The British Council moved into the Ministries of Education in a privileged position, as working colleagues. Often a British Council Officer would be posted to a Ministry as an Adviser or Curriculum Development Officer - and ODA found the funding for these members of staff in the Commonwealth as 'Aid to Commonwealth English' (ACE) or to 'Teaching of Science' (ACTS) officers (the Council career structure is still recovering from the imbalance created by the introduction of these cadres in the 'sixties). At the same time the Council undertook the administration of the British volunteer programme (principally VSOs), seeing to their placement and welfare at post. As volunteers were placed more and more in technical work and less in conventional grammar schools (which often fitted the aspirations of the volunteers and their sending institutions more than those of the receiving countries), so the Council in ex-colonies found its way into Ministries of Works, Survey, Agriculture or Transport.

By the 'seventies, VSO had become confident in its own abilities and gradually the Council shed its role as Overseas Aunt: the two organisations moved apart. But having achieved entrée to wider fields than education, the Council was ready to take on the whole task of Technical Co-operation Training. While in the UK its experience in student placement and welfare enabled it to receive the arriving trainee, the Representative overseas could deal directly with the manpower authorities overseas. The British Council working in a developing country is better placed to assess local needs than London-based aid officials; it can devote itself to establishing general mutualities while the latter must be concerned principally with ensuring the proper spending of the UK taxpayers' money and cannot easily identify itself with the country's cultural 'feel'. Moreover, it is in the cultural aspect of development that local Council staff can best presume their proper educational role - increasing knowledge and understanding about British culture in a way which is interactive rather than purely promotional.

British culture is itself becoming multi-cultural. This view was put to me by one Representative as a new strength on which to build. 'We should be conscious of our re-making of culture in the UK in order to export it.' For example, when British pop groups are sent to perform in Africa they are often a living example of this new multi-culturalism. At the same time they can help local musicians to reflect on their own identity as part of the local or national scene.

PROMOTING BRITAIN AND INCREASING 'INTER-NATIONAL UNDERSTANDING'?

A member of the Council's information department asserted to me quite categorically that the Council 'is not an altruistic organisation' and that constitutional references to international co-operation are to be seen as 'the last vestiges of altruism'. Perhaps: but it may also be the case that without a dash of altruism, effective 'promotion' would either not happen or be entirely counter-productive.

It can be argued that a central part of British culture is in fact its internationalism. The British Council abroad is very good at promoting this idea, particularly when the principle of mutuality is closely adhered to. But we have to ask ourselves whether, with our increasingly Eurocentric self-image, we are not helping to undermine the credibility of our own cultural agency in much of the developing world.

The major force of British cultural continuity abroad is in fact the Commonwealth and we neglect it only to our own disadvantage. The English language, British traditions of administration and justice, a developed education system, the usual range of sporting events; these are not only integral parts of British culture but are actively maintained by the Commonwealth and its members. And if British culture now contains a multi-cultural element it comes more from the Commonwealth than from any other source. The British Council will no doubt go on 'promoting Britain' as it has done so effectively for more than fifty years. Its history and present practice alike show that institutional autonomy, professional independence for its staff, adherence to mutuality and a sense of internationalism as part of British culture are all essential parts of this successful whole.

BIBLIOGRAPHY

Ashby, E. (Chairman) (1961), The Report of the Commission on Post-School Certificate and Higher Education in Nigeria (Government of Nigeria 1961)

British Council Annual Report 1951/52 (London: British Council)

British Council Annual Report 1986/87 (London: British Council)

Central Policy Review Staff (1977), Review of Overseas Representation (London: HMSO) (The Berrill Report)

Donaldson, F. (1984) The British Council: The First Fifty Years (London: Cape)

Duncan, V. (Chairman) (1969) Report of the Review Committee on Overseas Representation 1968-69, Cmnd 4107 (London: HMSO)

Fox, J. et al. (1987) Adult Educators from Africa: Issues in Training (Department of Adult Education, University of Southampton)

Hoggart, R. (1986) The British Council and the Arts: Activity Review No. 5 (London: British Council)

Mazrui, A. (1986) 'From the receiving end: a question of balance' in Britain Abroad No. 1 p. 5 (London: British Council)

Mitchell, J.M. (1986) International Cultural Relations (Allen and Unwin)

Seebohm, Lord et al. (1981) Review of the British Council (London: British Council) (The Seebohm Report)

Williams, P.R.C. (1985) They Came to Train (London: HMSO)

Chapter Three

THE BRITISH LIBRARY

Kenneth Cooper

INTRODUCTION

The British Library was established in 1973, by Act of Parliament in response to the recommendations of the National Libraries Committee. (1) By this measure a number of previously separate institutions were brought together under the management of the British Library Board, whose principal objectives (as set down in the Act) were 'to provide the best possible library service in the UK, to assume a position of leadership in library matters' and to make the Library 'a national centre for reference, study and bibliographical and other information services, in relation both to scientific and technological matters and to the humanities'.

The institutions concerned were the library departments of the British Museum, the National Central Library, the National Lending Library for Science and Technology, the British National Bibliography Limited, and the Office for Scientific and Technical Information. The largest unit of this group and the one with the longest history was the British Museum Library, with its origins in the British Museum Act of 1753 which charged the Museum to care for three important collections of books, manuscripts and papers (acquired by the State) and to make them available 'for publick use to all Posterity'. In 1960, the Museum had been entrusted with the National Reference Library for Science and Invention, which held the collections of the former Patent Office Library dating back to 1855, and so extended its subject coverage beyond the humanities and social sciences.

The National Central Library had been founded by the
Carnegie United Kingdom Trust in 1916 as the Central
Library for Students. It was renamed in 1931 when it was
given a Royal Charter as the official clearing house for
interlibrary loans. The National Lending Library for Science
and Technology was set up at Boston Spa in Yorkshire in
1962, initially with funding from the Department of
Scientific and Industrial Research (until the Department of
Education and Science took responsibility for it together
with the National Central Library in 1965). The British
National Bibliography had been set up by a non-profit
making consortium in 1949, while the Office for Scientific
and Technical Information was established to act as a small
research council within the Department of Education and
Science in 1965.

To these were added later the Library Association
Library (in 1974), the India Office Library and Records and
the HMSO Binderies (in 1982) and the British Institute of
Recorded Sound (in 1983, when it was renamed the National
Sound Archive). Full accounts of the history of the British
Library's constituent parts and of the events leading to its
formation can be found elsewhere. (2) While the formation
of a national library on the present pattern has taken place
comparatively recently the involvement of the State in this
area is of much longer standing.

When the Library was first formed the institutions
described above were organised in a structure consisting of
three operating Divisions (Reference, Lending and
Bibliographic Services) and two Departments (Central
Administration and Research and Development). In 1985,
following a major strategic planning exercise, the Library
was restructured into a Humanities and Social Sciences
division and a Science, Technology and Industry division (in
place of the former Reference and Lending Divisions) in
order to emphasise service provision to these leading
communities. A number of other changes were also made to
concentrate key policy responsibilities within the Library:
the Bibliographic Services division was given a Library-wide
responsibility for automation planning; a new directorate for
collection development was formed in Humanities and Social
Sciences; and a corporate marketing function was attached
to the Chief Executive's Office.

The British Library Board comprises a Chairman (part-
time), the Chief Executive, who is also Deputy Chairman,
the Directors General of the three operating divisions, and

nine other independent (part-time) members. Executive responsibility for day-to-day management of the Library rests with the three Directors General, the Director of the Research and Development Department and the Director of Central Administration, all of whom report to the Chief Executive.

The composition of the Board, with its mix of full-time and part-time members, is unusual and significant as one of two important provisions of the British Library Act designed to ensure that the new organisation did not become too inward-looking. Matters before the Board receive the attention not only of four senior executives from different parts of the Library, but also of ten independent persons, including industrialists, academics and senior members of the library profession. Moreover Section 2.3 of the Act enabled the Board to set up 'Advisory Councils with responsibility for providing advice to the Board, or to any department of the British Library, on such matters as the Secretary of State or the Board may determine from time to time', and from the outset great importance has been attached to both formal and informal consultative machinery, so that planning and performance are responsive to the needs of users. Soon after the formation of the British Library an Advisory Council was created 'to advise on the Library's relations with other libraries, both national and international, and on the character of the central services to be offered to the public', and shortly afterwards Advisory Committees were established for each of the main areas of operation.

Reference has already been made to the Library's responsibilities as set down in the Foundation Act. As part of the strategic planning exercise in 1985 the Board produced a formal definition of the <u>central aim</u> of the British Library:

> To preserve, develop, exploit and promote the combined resources of its collections and its facilities for reference, document supply, bibliographic, research, and other services for the best benefit, both now and in the future, of scholarship, research, industry, commerce and other major categories of information users. (3)

This statement of purpose was translated into a more detailed set of the Library's <u>functional objectives</u>, reproduced here in full to illustrate its wide-ranging involvement in the library and information network, which underpins its fundamental contribution to the cultural and economic life of the nation:

(i)   to ensure the availability of a comprehensive and permanent repository of recorded British material in all fields, published or otherwise;

(ii)   to ensure the availability of that foreign material which serves the needs at the national level for reference, study and information services;

(iii)   to provide a centralised document supply service;

(iv)   to provide the fullest possible range of information, bibliographic and other services to give effective access to the collections;

(v)   to create, distribute, and provide access to bibliographic records giving a comprehensive and continuous account of British and foreign publications;

(vi)   to keep abreast of other library, archive and information resources both at home and abroad, and to establish such cooperative arrangements as will give users direct access or other appropriate reference to the widest possible range of material;

(vii)   to identify priority needs for research and development in library, information and related activities; to provide support in these areas through funding research and demonstration projects; and to disseminate the results of research;

(viii) to assist those other libraries which are well placed to contribute significantly and at reasonable cost to the national collections as these are envisaged in (i) and (ii) above.

Of particular significance here is the extent to which the British Library's objectives go beyond those functions commonly associated with national libraries. These traditional functions typically comprise collecting comprehensively the nation's published output, conserving it, and creating records to form the national bibliography. Many national libraries operate as rather passive collections, available to the purposive reader for reference, but otherwise under-exploited. The British Library not only provides a centralised document supply service, which is extensively used in this country and abroad, but it also offers other services, such as online information retrieval, publishes bibliographies and scholarly works, and runs exhibitions, conferences and seminars. In addition, it supports research and development of benefit to the library and information community as a whole, provides financial assistance to other libraries with collections of national importance, and plays a leading role in co-operative initiatives in the UK, Europe and internationally.

In this way, the concepts of centralisation, leadership and service (foreshadowed in the opening paragraph) are in a very real sense translated into activities which make material contribution to scholarship, research, industry and commerce.

COLLECTIONS

'... a magnificent chronicle of human endeavour and imagination' Lord Dainton, Chairman, 1985.

The British Library's collections are an enormous national asset, providing an unparalleled resource for scholarship, research and industry. The collections include over 15.5 million volumes, 1 million discs and 40,000 hours of tape recordings. In addition to books, the holdings encompass manuscripts, maps, newspapers and other serials, patent specifications, stamps, music scores, sound recordings and trade literature.

The Humanities and Social Science division (formerly the Reference Division) holds more than 11 million volumes available for reference. Three individual collectors were responsible for the foundation collections of the British Museum's Library departments, and for establishing the precedents of bequests and donations which have brought the Museum and Library many valuable items over the years.

In 1753, Sir Hans Sloane, physician, amateur scientist, antiquarian and President of the Royal Society, bequeathed to the nation his collections of natural history, geological, zoological and medical phenomena, antiquities from Greece, Rome, Egypt and the Orient, drawings, coins and medals, and many books and manuscripts. Significantly it was this bequest which led to the establishment of the British Museum. The Government accepted the bequest and decided to house it with another state-owned collection of medieval manuscripts, cartularies, state papers and antiquities, built up by Sir Robert Cotton during the reign of Elizabeth I and James I and donated to the state by his grandson in 1700. The importance of the Cotton collection is indicated by the fact that it contained the Lindisfarne Gospels, two copies of the Magna Carta, and the manuscript of Beowulf. At this time the Government also purchased the collection of manuscripts, charters and rolls made by Robert Harley, first Earl of Oxford and one-time chief minister to Queen Anne, and his son, Edward, the second Earl.

In 1757, a fourth collection was added when George II donated to the Museum the Royal Library, begun in the 1470s by Edward IV and added to by succeeding monarchs. This gift brought to the Museum not only thousands of manuscripts and printed books, including the fifth-century Greek Codex Alexandrinus, but also the important right of copyright deposit, under the Act of 1709 which had provided that the Royal Library should receive one copy of every printed work registered at Stationers' Hall. The mechanism of legal deposit has made a major contribution to the growth of the collections over the years, and its current value to the Library has been estimated at over £1 million per annum. The tradition of bequests and donations has continued to the present day, a notable recent example being the gift in 1986 of the immensely valuable collection of autographs, musical and literary manuscripts formed by the Austrian writer Stefan Zweig.

The second half of the nineteenth century saw the rapid growth of several specialist collections in the Museum, such as those of maps, music and official papers. These collections have been developed and expanded over time, and today are still maintained as separate subject collections or libraries, with their own catalogues, reading rooms and other specialist services.

Descriptions of the collections, their richness and variety, can be found elsewhere, notably in the British Library Journal and in published guides. (4) However, it is worth noting here a few examples to give some indication of the scale of the Library's current operations. The English and European Language collections of printed books contain nearly 9 million volumes, including many rare and valuable early printed works as well as contemporary material. The Oriental Collections cover the languages and literatures of Asia and northern Africa. More than 40,000 volumes of manuscripts include religious, literary and historical works, illuminated Bibles, Gospels and Korans, and a collection of

Chinese Buddhist scrolls from Central Asia. There are over 640,000 printed books providing representative coverage of both modern and classical literature of the countries concerned, with an impressive collection of early imprints.

The British Library's collection of maps, both manuscript and printed, is the major cartographic resource in the country, and one of the most important in the world. The Map Library holds printed maps and charts, celestial and terrestrial globes. In addition, topographical maps and views and maritime charts are held in the King George III collections, and the manuscript maps inherited from the foundation collections of the Museum include much material from the medieval period. As well as items of historic interest, a wealth of modern maps, including remote sensing imagery is held.

The Philatelic collections have a broadly-based, international coverage with a diverse range of material embracing not only postage stamps but also revenue material, fiscal stamps and ephemera giving information on production, printing and design artists. Twenty-five large collections and a number of smaller ones are held, dating back to the mid-nineteenth century. The total number of items is estimated to be over 6 million.

The Library holds the national reference collections of manuscript and printed music and of sound recordings. In addition there are collections of music scores and other printed material available for loan. The collection of manuscript music amounts to some 10,000 volumes, containing more than an estimated 100,000 single items. The earliest musical manuscripts date from the Middle Ages, special treasures including the Old Hall Manuscript (early fifteenth century), the most important and comprehensive sources for the music of the Middle Ages and early Renaissance in England, and the 13th century song Sumer is i-cumen in. The collections are also strong in primary sources for the history of music in England from the 16th century to the present day. Many important European autographs are held, for example Haydn's 'Drum Roll' symphony, Mozart's ten great string quartets, and sketchbooks of Beethoven. Papers of musicians also feature, examples being those of Sir George Smart and, from this century, Sir Henry Wood.

Sound recordings are housed at the National Sound Archive (formerly the British Institute of Recorded Sound) in South Kensington, which was set up in 1950 and became a department of the British Library in 1983. The Archive has gathered and preserved a collection which reflects the development of recorded sound from early wax cylinders to modern compact discs. One of the earliest examples is a wax cylinder made in 1890 of Aboriginal chants, in the Torres Straits, Tasmania. Another is a recording of 'What the, How the, Who the, Where the' by the great music hall favourite Florrie Ford in 1915. The Archive attempts to acquire one copy of each disc issued commercially in the United Kingdom through voluntary deposit and encourages the deposit of private collections, as well as making its own recordings at outside venues. The collection is expanding by about 3,000 discs and 300 hours of tape a month. A large part is devoted to music in the Western concert tradition, but ethnic and folk music, popular music and jazz are also well represented. About twenty hours of BBC material is recorded by the Archive from broadcasts each week, and BBC Sound Archive discs and transcription service records are also held.

In addition to music, the Archive covers drama, spoken literature, sound effects, oral history, and documentary material. More than 500 recordings of public theatrical performances have been made in the last 25 years including as far as possible the complete repertories of the National Theatre, the Royal Shakespeare Company and (since 1973) the English Stage Company at the Royal Court. Fringe, provincial, touring and foreign theatre companies are represented in the collection, which also contains radio plays and interviews, as well as commercial discs of recorded drama. The Library of Wildlife Sounds has recordings of 5,000 animal species, including some of the earliest, such as that of a caged nightingale in 1905, thought to be the first recording of a bird ever made.

The Science, Technology and Industry division comprises the Science Reference and Information Service (SRIS, formerly the Science Reference Library) and the Document Supply Centre (DSC, formerly the British Library Lending Division). SRIS is the national library for modern science and technology, business and commerce, patents, trade marks and designs, and has the most comprehensive reference collection of such literature in Western Europe. In addition to nearly 200,000 books and pamphlets and over 30,000 current periodical titles, it holds 27 million patent specifications from many countries and a worldwide collection of related official gazettes, as well as directories, market surveys, trade literature and company information.

DSC has about 5 million books and serials and over 3 million documents in microform. It acquires significant books in English irrespective of subject and periodicals in all languages, as well as official publications of the UK and major intergovernmental organisations, report literature from more than 90 countries, conference proceedings, music scores, and British theses. (Virtually all UK universities and the Council for National Academic Awards supply their doctoral dissertations for filming.)

SERVICES

'To keep the publick stock of Learning, which is in Books and Manuscripts, to increas it, and to propose it to others in the waie which may be most helpful unto all' John Durie, Royal Librarian, 1650.

The Library exists for the benefit of current and future users; one of the key strategies identified in the corporate planning exercise was a major thrust towards developing a programme of wider service provision. The structure adopted by the Library at its inception emphasised its three main functions - reference, lending and bibliographic services. Over the past ten years, a number of factors have affected the basic pattern of service provision, notably the advent of new technology and the trend towards treating information as a tradable commodity, as well as other economic and social changes in the environment. The result has been considerable development and expansion of the range of services offered, coupled with a concerted effort to relate more closely to the needs of users. It was this which led to the restructuring of the Library in 1985 on a broad subject basis to distinguish between the provision of services to the Humanities and Social Sciences community on the one hand and to Science, Technology and Industry on the other.

Traditionally, national libraries have tended to emphasise resources not services, and effective use of the collections has largely depended on admission to reading rooms. In practice for the British Library this has meant that access to material has effectively been restricted (at least in Humanities and Social Sciences) to Reader's Pass holders who are able to visit the Library in person. Today access has been extended by some relaxation of the policy for admission to the Bloomsbury reading rooms, and also by improved provision of services to both visiting and remote users. The majority (approximately two thirds) of Bloomsbury readers are academics, of whom about half are postgraduate students and the rest are teaching staff. This underlines the central contribution the Library makes here to higher education. The balance is composed of librarians, information scientists, journalists, investigative professionals and others who need to use materials not readily available to them elsewhere. Around a third of Bloomsbury users are from overseas, the majority from the United States and other English-speaking countries. In addition to consulting material in the reading rooms, facilities available to users include reprographic services, offering photocopies, microfilm and photographs; and a computer search service, giving access to many humanities databases (including the post-1975 General Catalogue of printed books and the Eighteenth Century Short Title Catalogue).

The India Office Library and Records (IOLR, now part of the Collection Development directorate) has developed its services to education in recent years in response to the needs of local teachers. Work-packs have been produced for secondary school students, visits and seminars arranged for teachers and pupils, and a number of relevant publications issued. In 1986 a full-time Education Officer was appointed to oversee this work both for IOLR and the Oriental Manuscripts and Printed Books collections. The Library plans to extend services to schools throughout the division over the next few years.

The Document Supply Centre caters for remote user needs for humanities and social sciences material. It supplies loans, photocopies and microforms to other libraries and corporate organisations, both in this country and abroad - about half of DSC's customers are overseas, accounting for approximately a quarter of the total of requests received. In addition to satisfying requests from its own stock, it provides access to the holdings of public, academic and special libraries as the national centre for interlending within the UK and between the UK and countries overseas. New technology has brought improved services in this area, where requests can be accepted not only by mail, but also by telex, database hosts and DSC's own system ARTTel

(Automated Request Transmission by telephone). In addition various bespoke services have been developed including an Urgent Action Service with the option of a telefacsimile response. Services available from the National Sound Archive (NSA) include the transcription of deleted commercial discs (subject to copyright clearance). The listening service, available by appointment to any member of the public, is now available both at the Archive's premises in South Kensington and in the DSC reading room at Boston Spa, in Yorkshire. In addition, NSA has a comprehensive library, and an information service which can assist with preliminary research to locate particular recordings and can advise on their availability and on manufacturers' or distributors' addresses. It also holds regular series of discussion evenings and lectures, which cover artistic, technical and scientific aspects of sound recordings.

Within the Science, Technology and Industry division, a range of services to meet more specialised information requirements has been developed, in addition to general enquiry services backed up by the computer search service, which provides access to over 150 databases around the world. A notable example is the Japanese Information Service, which provides access to Japanese scientific, technological and industrial information and acts as a referral service, as well as offering online searching and linguistic aid. The division also holds seminars on exploitation of the literature in a number of subject areas, such as business information and industrial property and courses on how to use the document supply services to best effect.

Another service which has developed in recent years is the Library's publishing programme. Annual turnover now exceeds £3 million. There are currently more than 400 titles in print covering a wide variety of books and journals, ranging from specialist reference works to a new series of illustrated paperbacks intended to introduce the general reader to the collections. Bibliographical aids, catalogues, guides and manuscript facsimiles feature in the published list.

Serials, in both hard copy and microform, account for a substantial part of the output, examples to note including the annual Current Research in Britain (formerly Research in British Universities, Polytechnics and Colleges) the monthly Index of Conference Proceedings Received, and the twice-yearly British Library Journal, which carries scholarly articles by Library staff and other authorities on the collections.

In February 1987 one of the largest retrospective publishing projects ever undertaken was launched by the British Library in collaboration with a commercial publisher, to make available on microfiche a scholarly selection of nineteenth century books and pamphlets held by major research libraries in Britain and the USA. The publication programme of some 250,000 titles will be carried out over 30 years, with texts issued as part of a large General Collection (covering the social sciences, history, science and technology) or as part of separately available Specialist Collections (in Linguistics; Publishing, the Booktrade and the Diffusion of Knowledge; Visual Arts and Architecture; Literature; and Music). The Nineteenth Century will provide scholars with an unrivalled source of essential texts for the understanding of the political, social, economic, ethical and intellectual changes of the period. Many of the works concerned are now urgently in need of preservation and their republication in microform will enable access without further damage to the originals.

A function of the Library not explicitly stated in its objectives is that of the national museum of the book as an artefact. In fulfilling this role the Exhibitions and Education Service mounts permanent and temporary displays of some of the Library's outstanding items in the public exhibition galleries in Bloomsbury, and also arranges gallery talks, lectures and audiovisual presentations. Many of the temporary exhibitions are given permanent form through publication of accompanying catalogues.

The Bibliographic Services division provides a range of products in direct support of the library, information and publishing communities, and of ultimate benefit to both the academic world and the industrial sector. Its primary activity is the creation of a national database recording the UK published output, derived from material received under the terms of the Copyright Act of 1911 (as amended by the British Library Act 1972). A range of printed and microfiche bibliographies are published, including the British National Bibliography and Books in English; and the records created are also made available on magnetic tape in machine-readable form and online through the BLAISE-LINE service. This central resource is extensively used, by libraries and others, for book selection and acquisition, information retrieval and cataloguing.

A major project now under way is the computerisation of the Library's 8 million-entry General Catalogue, which is being undertaken in association with an outside contractor. On completion the machine readable catalogue will be amongst the largest single bibliographic databases in the world and will enable direct online access for users of the Library's reading rooms. It is also intended to publish the converted catalogue on compact disc or other optical storage media.

Another recent initiative has been the publication of a list of the book holdings of the Document Supply Centre. Books at Boston Spa lists all the English language titles and Western European Language books with a publication date of 1980 or later. The initial list contained 265,000 titles, with 5,000 being added every month. The listing has been made available both on microfiche and through BLAISE-LINE, which enables DSC users to request material online simply by using the special ORDER! command.

CO-OPERATION

'Across the whole range of services there must be a partnership between the British Library and the other library services of this country. It is not just up to the Board - it is up to us to see that this partnership continues and provides the basis for the best library service in the world.' D.T. Richnell, Goldsmiths' Librarian, 1973

Among the Library's stated objectives is that of keeping abreast of other library, archive and information resources both at home and abroad, and establishing such co-operative arrangements as will give users direct access or other appropriate reference to the widest possible range of material. It has already been noted that the provisions relating to the composition of the British Library Board and the establishment of the Advisory Committees were two means of ensuring an outgoing attitude. The Library has important relations with and responsibilities towards other libraries and consultation is an essential characteristic of its method of operation.

Alongside the Advisory Committees, there are many ad hoc committees, discussion groups and working parties, whose membership spans, in addition to the library and information community, the academic world, the book trade, commerce and industry as appropriate. A typical instance of this mode of working is the ongoing series of colloquia initiated by the Library to bring together scholars, librarians, diplomats, members of the business community and others to consider the use and development of resources and services in particular areas or languages with a view to initiating future co-operative ventures. Two recent examples are those on German language resources and on African studies; both sets of papers were subsequently published. (5)

In turn, the Library is represented on the committees and working groups of other organisations, notably those of the Standing Conference of National and University Libraries (SCONUL), which has made a valuable contribution to improving co-operation in fields such as Latin American and Asian studies, and the University of London Library Resources Co-ordinating Committee.

The British Library is also represented on the Library and Information Services Council (LISC) which advises the Minister for the Arts on library and information matters, and has through its working parties contributed to the ongoing professional debate on co-operation and interaction. Examples here include the development of the concept of Library and Information Plans (LIPs) for local authority areas and an examination of public-private sector relationships in library and information service provision, with the Library's Research and Development Department closely involved in both these areas.

These formal arrangements for representation and collaboration are but a small part of the more informal network of relationships which the staff of the British Library enjoy and set out to maintain with all who have a serious interest in creating, collecting, organising, disseminating and using the growing stock of literature of all kinds, especially for purposes of research and further development.

The practical manifestations of co-operative activity can be seen in many areas. While the mutual dependence of libraries in the UK has long been recognised, the incentive to share resources more effectively and to engage in joint ventures has increased with the reductions in funding experienced by libraries and education in recent years.

The Library's Document Supply Centre has always

worked closely with its 'back-up' libraries and the regional library bureaux and has long played a major role in national co-ordination and planning for interlending, for example in the support of regional union holdings lists and in the development of rail/road transport schemes for interlibrary loans. On behalf of the UK, DSC is one of the main participants in the European Communities-sponsored System for Information on Grey Literature in Europe (SIGLE) which aims to improve both bibliographic control and physical availability of reports, theses, proceedings, teaching notes, working papers etc (and is now accessible to universities and other libraries via BLAISE-LINE). In response to budget cuts in university libraries, DSC maintains a file of all serial titles cancelled by British universities and takes this into account in its own serials acquisition policy.

A good example of a formalised co-operative arrangement is the Patents Information Network (PIN) developed by the Science Reference and Information Service as a means of providing access to patent information, related journals and indexes (and in some cases actual specifications) through designated major public libraries. More informal is the co-operation between the Business Information Service (at SRIS) and the City Business Library and the Department of Trade's Statistics and Market Intelligence Library, as a basis for the reference and referral service intended to support other libraries in London and the provinces.

On the humanities side, an agreement to co-ordinate collecting policies was made in 1986 between IOLR, OMPB and the University of London's School of Oriental and African Studies (which built on a previous arrangement between IOLR and SOAS predating the former's entry into the British Library). A pre-requisite for any large-scale approach to co-ordinated collection development is information on the scope of existing collections, including current collecting policies. The British Library has taken the lead in this area first by publishing a broad outline to its collection development priorities, (6) and then by compiling detailed schedules indicating its approach to collecting by subject, using a technique known as 'Conspectus' (developed in the United States by the Research Libraries Group). This technique provides sufficient detail to allow the librarian or reader to understand the scope of a particular collection, or part of a collection, and to appreciate the limitations which the library is imposing in its acquisition of a particular subject. Furthermore, it has the potential to enable libraries to develop strategies for resource-sharing based on up-to-date knowledge of acquisition policies and collection strengths in other libraries, as well as facilitating effective co-operative collection development and conservation on a regional, national or international basis.

Another area where the Library has taken the lead and fostered co-operation is in preservation, where the scale of the problem facing the library community is enormous. In the British Library alone, it has been estimated that some 1.65 million volumes need treatment and the number is rising all the time. In 1984, following a major research report and subsequent consultation with the library community, the National Preservation Office (located within the Library's Preservation Service) and a National Preservation Advisory Committee were established. The Office promotes awareness, provides information and initiates debates on national issues, as well as encouraging co-operative ventures. In the first phase of its programme it has produced a video programme, Keeping your words, a 'Preservation survival kit' and a series of posters and bookmarks for use in libraries and schools.

Recognising the potential economies to be made through co-operation in the large-scale microfilming of material for preservation (and the benefits to collection development and document supply services) the Library has initiated a number of collaborative projects of this type. A major example is the NEWSPLAN programme for microfilming UK provincial newspapers. This began with a pilot project in the South West of England, and was then extended to other areas with the aim eventually to make all local and regional newspapers in the country available. A National Register of Microform Masters has been established to support a co-ordinated approach to filming both in this country and abroad.

Since 1974 one of the means by which the British Library has ensured the availability of research level material has been through the awarding of grants to other libraries for conservation, cataloguing and improving access to collections of national importance. Section 1.3(b) of the British Library Act enables the Board to do this, and over the years several million pounds have been granted for a wide range of projects. To give but one example, substantial help has been given to the Bibliographical Society to complete the union catalogue of pre-1701 books in cathedral libraries of England and Wales. Awards have also been made for the purchase of important heritage items to add to existing collections. (7)

Interlibrary co-operation is an area where the Library's Research and Development Department has funded a programme of linked projects to help the library community towards greater efficiency in the use of resources. The Department currently commits some £1.5 million a year in grants for research and development in all subject fields directed to the benefit of the national library and information system as a whole. Its priorities for research over the period 1985-90 are information technology, including electronic publishing and library automation; industrial, commercial and business information; information policy; and basic and strategic research (examining the underlying principles of information storage and retrieval).

In 1986 a major three-year project was launched aimed at improving the speed and efficiency of information exchange in research communities, with work being carried out at Hatfield Polytechnic, the Universities of Birmingham and Loughborough, and University College London (under the title 'Project Quartet'). The research involves the technologies of computer networking, mass data storage and retrieval (in the form of text, picture and graphics) and visual display techniques, aiming to develop a single integrated information storage and retrieval system for the benefit of academic researchers. At the other end of the spectrum the Department has supported work involving school children in its user education programme, which has contributed to changes in information handling skills and teaching methods. And a project that has made a substantial impact on the general public is the Public Information in Rural Areas Technology Experiment (PIRATE) which involved the use of a network of microcomputers to provide a community information service in North Devon.

In addition to funding specific projects and programmes, the Department has supported research centres based at universities or polytechnics to provide a focus for work in a particular area. Current examples are the Centre for Bibliographic Management at the University of Bath, the Library and Information Technology Centre at the Polytechnic of Central London and the Office for Humanities Communication at the University of Leicester. The latter was established in 1982 and has three main spheres of activity - research, liaison and dissemination of information. Its research effort is directed towards the systematic study of the communication of information in the humanities in the UK, with particular reference to computer applications. There is an active programme of liaison with scholars, libraries, publishers, learned societies and relevant bodies such as funding agencies in the UK, North America and Western Europe, with a view to engaging in joint research and educational activities where feasible. The Office promotes awareness of developments in humanities communication through meetings, conferences, demonstrations, a printed newsletter and an online bulletin board. Examples of meetings held in the past two years include a colloquium on computer applications to medieval studies, and seminars on computer applications to musical analysis and on text processing and the production of scholarly manuscripts.

The Research and Development Department also administers the British National Bibliography Research Fund, which was set up in 1975 when the assets of BNB Ltd were transferred to the British Library, and exists to support research into book trade and related library activities. In recent years resources have been concentrated on the impact of new technologies on the publication chain, as well as continuing earlier work investigating the reading habits of various sectors of society. In common with other projects supported by the Department, the results of major studies are formally published in a series of research reports.

Co-operation thus extends beyond the library and information network to the book world including the publishing community. The Library (itself a publisher and member of the Publishers Association) works closely with UK publishers on matters of common interest such as the Cataloguing-in-Publication programme. Over 1,000 publishers now participate in this scheme, which provides advance information on forthcoming British books for incorporation in the British National Bibliography to the mutual benefit of the book trade, libraries and readers. A more recent initiative has been the development of a statement on permanent (acid-free) paper, jointly sponsored by the National Preservation Office, the Library Association and the Publishers Association, and addressed to British publishers to enlist their support in encouraging the production and use of such paper.

The Library also co-operates with commercial partners in joint publishing ventures, including books, facsimile reproductions and microforms (as in the case of The Nineteenth Century). Together with the Department of Trade and Industry and Publishers Databases Limited, it is involved in an experiment known as the 'Knowledge Warehouse' project designed to gain practical experience of the archiving of electronic publications. In the world of sound, the NSA has reached an agreement with the Mechnical-Copyright Protection Society for the establishment of a National Discography, which by 1990 will have developed a database containing relevant information about all current sound recordings widely available in the UK.

In the area of non-book materials - films, video recordings, photographs, slides and so on - the Library has no direct responsibility for collecting. But recognising that these materials are as much a part of the nation's culture and heritage as printed matter, it has co-operated with bodies concerned with the different media to establish a national forum to consider issues of common concern, such as archival arrangements and bibliographical control.

The international dimension of the Library's sphere of operations has been indirectly mentioned in the context of particular activities. It is a significant part of the Library's responsibilities (both on its own behalf and for others in the United Kingdom) to maintain effective contact with main library and information developments in other countries and at international level. As one of the world's greatest research libraries with worldwide collections and readers the Library recognises the need to maintain bilateral links of comparable scope.

Thus, for many years the Library has played an active part in the International Federation of Library Associations and Institutions (IFLA), not only through staff participation in its Standing Committees, but also by housing three of its core programmes. And it has recently assumed responsibility for the UK membership of the International Federation for Documentation (FID). Active links exist with other organisations concerned to promote interlibrary co-operation, particularly at the European level and with North America.

Examples of co-operative activity include a dedicated transatlantic telecommunications link established with initial connections to the US Research Libraries Group's network (RLIN) and the National Library of Medicine's medical databases, and the agreements reached for the exchange of records with the Library of Congress, the Bibliotheque Nationale and other leading national libraries. Underpinning these initiatives are the important working relationships established by many staff at operational level with their counterparts abroad.

A unique example of British-American co-operation can be seen in the American Trust for the British Library, which was formed in 1979 with the aim of enhancing the Library's American collections, primarily by purchasing materials to fill identified weaknesses in the collections for the period 1880-1950. The acquisition of American material is supported by donations from corporations and foundations, and through subscriptions from Associates of the Trust. The Trust also has a role in conservation through identifying locations of out-of-print desiderata and arranging for them to be microfilmed.

Finally, it must not be forgotten that because of its history the Library is effectively a second national library to many countries of the former Empire - as well as others - with which co-operative projects are a regular feature of operations (notably to make good deficiencies in their archives by microfilming). The Library also plays a role in national overseas development policy by sharing its experience with developing countries. In this it works closely with the British Council, both in supplying staff to work on short term consultancies overseas and in receiving a steady stream of visitors to the Library as part of its contribution to cultural diplomacy and education.

RESOURCES

While the Library's collections are its greatest assets, the value of those assets could not begin to be preserved or realised without the expertise and commitment of the staff. Many of the Library's activities are inescapably labour-intensive and the effective provision of services is entirely dependent on those who are responsible for their management and operation. Over and above the concern for effectiveness in carrying out its basic activities, the Library has to ensure the maintenance of that scholarly tradition on which its usefulness, development and reputation as a great research library ultimately depends.

Staff development was treated as an important issue in the Library's Strategic Plan, where it was recognised that there was a need to foster relevant staff scholarship, to encourage greater flexibility and to develop management, marketing and computing skills. These requirements help to shape the Library's internal management and training programmes, and following the Strategic Plan, a policy statement was produced which set out to elucidate facilities and opportunities available for staff to keep abreast of their subject interests and to undertake bibliographical and other research. The evidence of staff scholarship can typically be seen in their publications, whether issued by the Library or elsewhere.

Accommodation is currently a major problem for the Library, which is at present a multi-site operation occupying some 20 buildings in the London area, as well as the complex in West Yorkshire. Its stock extends to over 360 miles of shelving, growing at the rate of 8 miles every year. Most important of all is the fact that its existing locations do not provide the environmental conditions required to preserve the collections for future users.

In 1980 the Government authorised the construction of the first phase of a new building for the Library on a site adjacent to St Pancras station. The new building has been designed to overcome the problems of crowded reading rooms, multi-site storage, outhousing of material and poor environmental conditions. It will eventually enable the Library to preserve, manage, exploit and present the national collections more effectively for the benefit of future users. Among the benefits will be more open access, fuller use of new technology, and better space for exhibitions and a bookshop to allow the Library's treasures to be more widely appreciated. The St Pancras building is one of the largest public building projects of the twentieth century. Estimated costs of the work to be completed by 1993 (Stage 1A) total over £200 million (at 1986 prices). By then, in addition to atmospherically-controlled storage for the Library's collections, there will be reading rooms for rare books, music and science, and an exhibition gallery. Further provisions, including general reading rooms for the humanities and social sciences, will depend on later stages of the building which have yet to be approved.

The Library is financed by an annual grant-in-aid from Government, and also generates substantial income by the sale of services and publications. After initial growth during the Library's formative period, the real value of the grant-in-aid has been reduced over the past six years. While strenuous and successful efforts have been made to market existing services, introduce new ones and generate higher revenue, the resources available for maintaining the currency of the collections and preserving them have inevitably fallen.

In 1983 the Minister for the Arts said that libraries in general should look beyond their traditional sources of funds, and specifically asked the British Library 'to give careful consideration to the possibility of attracting private resources so as to maintain and develop new ways of exploiting the Library's collections and services for the general benefit ...'. (8) The Library has been fortunate over the years in receiving a number of substantial gifts, a recent example being the £1 million from the Wolfson Foundation and Family Trust, which enabled the Board to restore and extend the awarding of grants to institutions with collections of national importance (following a moratorium on such grants, imposed in 1984/5 owing to a lack of resources). More concerted efforts are now being made to obtain such assistance, and in particular to attract sponsorship from business and industry.

An important set of pricing policies for services has also been developed which distinguishes different categories of activities and appropriate levels of charging, depending on the extent to which activities are regarded as a 'public good' or as tailored to meeting the more closely defined needs of particular users. In this overall context the British Library Board has taken the firm view that no charge should be made for admission to its reading rooms. The Board sets store by the civilised tradition of free access for researchers to published knowledge. At the same time the Library is charging for 'premium services' which make heavy demands on staff time.

The Strategic Plan recognised that the Library's ability to carry out its programme would depend on both its own efforts at self-help - increasing revenue, working with the private sector and attracting sponsorship - and continued level funding by Government. The Plan also gave a commitment to earmark a fixed proportion of the budget for expenditure on acquisitions as a core priority. Even so the number of new purchases and the proportion of the world's published output which the Library is able to acquire is declining steadily, with book and periodical prices rising above the general rate of inflation and the number of new titles growing each year. The situation is further affected by fluctuating exchange rates and increased competition for 'heritage' items at auctions, particularly from overseas, all at a time when other institutions in the UK are suffering similar problems and demanding more of the national library as a result.

CONCLUSION

By any standards the British Library is a rich resource for researchers and other users whether in the humanities or the sciences, and has great potential for setting new patterns of operation and leading or enabling new initiatives to be taken at a time when the value of information is seen to be appreciating in almost every area of life. Over the past ten years or so the Library has achieved a good deal in pursuit of its statutory obligations to make services available to institutions of education and learning, other libraries and industry, and contribute to the efficient management of other libraries and information services. But there is still much more to be done.

The British Museum Library was in many respects a book and manuscript museum, a reference and research library, whose primary obligation was to the scholarly community. It was seen by some as elitist and inward-looking; to others it seemed remote and out of touch; its function was very much that of custodian rather than disseminator. Since its formation the British Library, having brought together the library departments of the Museum with several very different institutions, has set out to build on the combined strengths of the various parts to produce an organisation which is more accessible, co-operative, and above all responsive to the needs of its users and to changes in its environment.

The Government's commitment to providing a new building at St Pancras is at once a powerful incentive and a strong guarantee for the role of the national library to be developed to meet the changing expectations and opportunities that lie ahead. That development will also depend on the adequacy of resources available for maintaining and preserving the collections, for exploiting information technology, for staffing the Library across the wide range of its activities. Clearly the overall level of resources available to the British Library is dependent, like so many other things, upon the level of prosperity of the nation. What is less well understood is that the converse is also true: the scale of annual financial support for the British Library will bear not only on the effectiveness of the national library and information system as a whole, but also on the future economic and cultural achievements of the United Kingdom.

Entrusted with the record of creative thinking and writing which has inspired and informed the development of Western civilisation, the Library has a duty to continue the traditions of its forebears and stimulate the progress of future generations. The Library is, indeed, a unique product of both the glory and the wealth of Britain's past; it has a distinctive role to play in helping present and future generations both to sustain civilised values and generate new wealth.

NOTES

1. National Libraries Committee. Report. Cmnd 4028.
2. See Bibliography.
3. Advancing with Knowledge, p. 13.
4. Notable acquisitions are also listed each year in the Library's Annual Report.
5. British Library Paper No. 8. ISBN 0 7123 0096 1 and British Library Paper No. 6. ISBN 0 7123 0050 3.
6. Advancing with Knowledge, pp. 19-20.
7. Grants made to other libraries are listed in the Annual Report.
8. Report by the Minister for the Arts on library and information matters during 1983. (Cmnd. 9109).

BIBLIOGRAPHY

Advancing with knowledge: The British Library strategic plan 1985-1990. London: The British Library Board, 1985

British librarianship today ed. W.L. Saunders. London: Library Association, 1976, e.g. ch. 4, The British Library: an introduction; ch. 5, The British Library Reference Division; ch. 6, The British Library Lending

Division; ch. 7, The British Library Bibliographic
Services Division; ch. 8. The British Library Research
and Development Department
The British Library: the Reference Division collections ed.
Janice Anderson. London: The British Library, 1983
Esdaile, Arundel. The British Museum Library: a short
history and survey. London: Allen and Unwin, 1946
Filon, S.P.L. The National Central Library: an experiment in
library co-operation. London: Library Association, 1977
Houghton, Bernard. Out of the dinosaurs the evolution of the
National Lending Library for Science and Technology.
London: Bingley, 1972
Jones, Graham. The making of the British Library. Library
Review, 32(1) Spring 1983, 7-31
Miller, Edward. That noble cabinet: a history of the
British Museum. London: Deutsch, 1973
OSTI - the first five years: the work of the Office of
Scientific and Technical Information, 1965-70. London:
HMSO, 1971
Ratcliffe, F.W. Preservation policies and conservation in
British libraries: report of the Cambridge University
Library conservation project. London: British Library,
1984 (LIR report 25)
Wells, A.J. New patterns in bibliographic services: the role
of the Bibliographic Services Division of the British
Library. In: Proceedings, papers and summaries of
discussions at the Public Libraries Conference held at
Aberdeen, 11th September to 19th September 1974.
London: Library Association, 1974, 53-8
Wilson, Alex. The incorporation of the British Museum
Library into the British Library In: Studies in library
management, 7 ed. Anthony Vaughan. London: Bingley,
1982, 167-91

Chapter Four

THE BRITISH MUSEUM

John Reeve

The British Museum is not a Government department, but a quango. There is no state museum service, as in France, many Third World countries, or eastern Europe. The Museum (founded in 1753) has received public funding since 1762, and today receives over 13 million pounds per annum via the Office of Arts and Libraries, for staff and running costs. The Museum increasingly has to turn to sponsors for activities as varied as fieldwork, publications, video, new galleries and exhibitions. The Director is accountable to Parliament - like his precedessors - and may be summoned to appear before relevant Select Committees. Until 1963 the Archbishop of Canterbury, the Lord Chancellor and the Speaker of the House of Commons were ex officio the three Principal Trustees. The Prime Minister today appoints 15 of the 25 Trustees, the rest being appointed either by learned societies, the Crown or the Trustees themselves. Today they include a former cabinet minister as chairman, a former Director General of the BBC, heads of three Oxbridge colleges, the managing director of GEC, the sculptor Dame Elisabeth Frink, and as Royal Trustee the Duke of Gloucester. The Museum staff are employed by the Trustees, but their conditions of employment are identical with the Civil Service.

THE MUSEUM AND ITS PUBLIC ROLE

The Act of 1753 setting up the Museum outlines its purpose:

> therefore ... not only for the inspection and

entertainment of the learned and the curious, but for the general use and benefit of the public; may ... it be enacted that within London or Westminster ... one general repository shall be erected ... for public use to all posterity. (26 Geo II c. 22)

The problem of identifying 'the public' and deciding how to deal with its needs had begun. Although the British Museum has been hailed as 'the first national, public, secular museum' in the world, its concept of public was at first limited. A written application had to be made for an admission ticket, and ticket holders were then admitted in restricted numbers. Parties of five at a time were taken round, often at breakneck speed:

so rapid a passage through a vast suite of rooms in little more than 1 hour of time ... confuses, stuns and overpowers the visitor. (Caygill 1981:13)

The experience of that German tourist in 1782 is repeated daily by tour groups throughout the summer.

Despite the restrictions, by 1784 the visitors to the Museum were said to consist 'chiefly of mechanics and persons of the lower classes', some of whom could acquire tickets from ticket touts for two shillings. Tickets were abolished in 1805, and after 1810 'persons of decent appearance' could even wander around unescorted on certain days.

The presence of 'the general public' in the Museum did not please Sir Henry Ellis, Domesday scholar and Principal Librarian (i.e. Director), who informed the 1835 Select Committee on the Museum:

People of a higher grade would hardly wish to come to the Museum at the same time with sailors from the dockyards and girls whom they might bring with them. I do not think such people would gain any improvement from the sight of our collections. (Caygill 1981:25)

In 1835 the Museum had 289,104 visitors. In a letter to a newspaper Ellis asserted that the Museum was:

maintained for many laudable purposes, among which the merely popular one of mingled amusement and instruction to those persons who walk through it is by no means the chief. (ibid.)

Parliament took a different view:

> That the great accessions which have been made of late
> to the collections of the British Museum, and the
> increasing interest taken in them by the public render it
> expedient to revise the Establishment of the Institution
> with a view to place it upon a scale more
> commensurate with, and better adapted to the present
> state and future prospects of the Museum. (Denvir
> 1984:187)

Benjamin Hawes, MP for Lambeth, led the pressure for
the British Museum to open on holidays. (He also helped to
found the Royal Fine Arts Commission in 1841.) In spite of
Sir Henry Ellis, 23,895 visitors came to the Museum on
Easter Monday 1837, the first public holiday on which it was
open. The most popular objects were birds, minerals, Magna
Carta and, rather surprisingly, antiquities from Mexico and
Peru. An important exhibition of Mexican antiquities and
natural history had been held in the Egyptian Hall in
Piccadilly in 1824, collected by William Bullock, 'assisted by
the government of that country' (Denvir 1984: 194).

MPs in particular were very concerned about the role of
museums in improving public taste. A member of the 1853
Select Committee, Richard Moncton Milnes, asked Sir
Richard Westmacott, professor at the Royal Academy and
sculptor of the pediment of the British Museum, about the
impact on public taste of 'earlier and Oriental art' (i.e. Near
Eastern as well as Chinese), as opposed to classical, which
was still widely regarded as the best model for artist and
public alike.

> 'Do you think there is no fear that introducing freely
> into the institution objects of more occasional and
> peculiar interest, such for instance as the sculptures
> from Nineveh, may deteriorate the public taste, and
> less incline them than they otherwise would be to study
> works of great antiquity and great art?'

> 'I think it impossible that any artist can look at the
> Nineveh marbles as works for study, for such they
> certainly are not; they are works of prescriptive art,
> like works of Egyptian art. No man would think of

67

studying Egyptian art.' 'Have not cases occurred in the intellectual history of many nations, in which the very free introduction of more barbarious specimens, such, for instance, as the Chinese, have had a very injurious effect upon taste in general?' 'I certainly think that the less people, as artists, look at objects of that kind the better,' Westmacott replied. (Haskell 1976:54-5)

By 1863 Alexander Beresford Hope MP, later PRIBA and Trustee of the British Museum, was telling a Royal Commission:

> Men who were mere workmen a few years ago are getting more and more artistic with the growth of public taste. (Pearson 1982:11)

Senior curators also felt concerned about the educational role of the Museum: Ellis, despite his views on the public, had written popular guidebooks.

Dr Samuel Birch, Keeper of Oriental Antiquities (i.e. Egypt, Near East) 1860-65, had this ambitious view of the British Museum's educational role, according to his son:

> Dr Birch was one of those who saw in the British Museum ... not only a storehouse of historical treasures ... not only a show-place for holiday recreation of the masses ... not only the conventional appendage of imperial greatness, but the true and indispensable home of the proficient master, and the proper and constant resort of the enquiring student: a university, in fact, where education in the most recondite branches of knowledge should be bountifully bestowed on all those who sought it, a centre to which all historical and scientific research should naturally gravitate. (James 1981:14)

Panizzi, Principal Librarian 1856-66 saw the national library existing 'for the furtherance of education, for study and research', where a poor student could 'have the same means of indulging his learned curiosity as the richest man in the country.' (Francis 1971:18)

One of the greatest Victorian pioneers in art and design education was Sir Henry Cole, the first director of the Victoria and Albert Museum, opened in the 'Brompton Boilers' in 1857. It was the Victoria and Albert Museum, and not the British Museum which was to become the Workshop of the World's 'Museum of Manufactures', or 'Museum of Ornamental Art' as it had variously been described. As Sir Roy Strong, a recent Director, has rather wearily observed,

> the pull between a practical museum of the arts of manufacture and design, with its aim to educate the masses, as against a museum of masterpieces, the resort of antiquarians and connoisseurs, has never been resolved to this day. (Strong 1977:4)

Today the collections of the Victoria and Albert Museum and the British Museum largely complement each other in common areas of collecting: both have important Oriental collections, but only the Victoria and Albert Museum collects oriental textiles and furniture. The major Eumorfopoulos Collection of Chinese art, for example, was shared between the two museums.

The Victoria and Albert Museum is still much more closely associated with art and design education than the British Museum, though secondary school art and design education is now one of the fastest growing areas of the British Museum Education Service's work. The Victoria and Albert Museum, with extensive collections from Chaucer's time to Scott Fitzgerald's, is also able to tailor-make courses to English examination set books. Without mummies, moon dust or dinosaurs, it is not, however, currently used by large numbers of primary school children, in the way that the British Museum or the Science and Natural History Museums are.

In 1870 the Metropolitan Museum of Art was founded in New York with the intention, like the Victoria and Albert Museum, of 'encouraging and developing the study of the fine arts, and the application of the arts to manufacture ... of furnishing popular instruction and recreation.' One trustee declared that 'every nation that has tried it has found that wise investment in the development of art pays more than compound interest.' By 1905 there were weekend lectures at The Met, and public school teachers were allowed to bring in students and use a classroom set aside for them. Francis Henry Taylor (Director 1940-54) wanted The Met to become 'a free and informal liberal arts college', abolished the entrance fee and established the Junior museum. Like the Louvre, but unlike the British Museum, The Met has a major collection of paintings as well as antiquities and decorative arts. Much of The Met's educational work is funded either by individual sponsors, or by combinations of state, federal and private money. (Hibbard 1980: 8, 19, 574)

The British Museum has combined from the outset the features of the 18th century learned society and later academic institutions with the public role of display and education. It is still the most popular museum in Britain, with circa 4 million visitors a year. It is the most popular free attraction in Britain after Blackpool Pleasure Beach. But the Museum's twin functions of research and display do not seem to have become as separated as at the Natural History Museum, which received the British Museum's natural history collections in 1883, and is now quite independent. There the Public Services Department has evolved galleries akin to an American Science Centre, concept - rather than object - based. As in some leading American museums, the displays are interactive, they are evaluated and then redisplayed in the light of that evaluation. (Miles and Alt 1982)

By 1878 the British Museum was open every day except Sunday. Since 1896 it has opened on Sunday afternoons, but not after 5.00 p.m. on weekday evenings, except for special lectures or private views. In this it is like most museums in Britain, but unlike many American museums, or the Centre Pompidou in Paris, for example. Working people therefore have to come either at weekends, when the Museum is often crowded, or rush in to lunchtime lectures if they work locally, as up to 200 people may, from Tuesday to Saturday. Opening hours were one aspect of national museums recently criticised by the FDA, the union to which senior museum staff belong, in its 1987 report 'A Stitch in Time'.

Two visitor surveys help us to assess the nature of the British Museum's public. In 1971, Peter Wingfield Digby carried out visitor surveys at the British Museum, the Science Museum and the National Maritime Museum. The differences were considerable: only 18% of British Museum visitors were under the age of 16 (National Maritime Museum - 40%, Science Museum - 48%); the British Museum had the highest proportion of visitors still in some form of post-secondary education (13%), and visitors to all three museums had received far more formal education than the general population, the British Museum's visitors to a greater extent than the other two. British Museum visitors were more specific about what they had come to see (11%

specified Egypt), but 54% still said they were 'planning to
have a general look round'. Twenty-three per cent of visitors
to the British Museum said they had been at least ten times
before, 47% were first-timers - predominantly either
tourists or school children. (Wingfield Digby, 1974: vii; 25;
57; viii)

In 1982-83, Peter Mann carried out a much fuller survey
- just on the British Museum. It revealed just how
international the Museum's public had become: half the
winter visitors were foreign, as much as three-quarters in
the summer. About two-thirds of the UK visitors were from
London and the southeast. The predominant age groups,
other than schools, were adults between the ages of 20 and
39. Between 53% and 66% of adult visitors belonged to
social class AB (managerial and professional), between 24%
and 37% to C1 (clerical, technical, white collar). 45% out of
the 61% who read a daily paper took The Times, Daily
Telegraph or The Guardian. Between 36% and 48% of
visitors finished their education at above the age of 22.
Nearly a quarter of visitors in term time were college or
university students. As in 1971, Egypt was the area most
specified by visitors, although 13% cited the current
Japanese exhibition as the reason for their visit. (Mann
1986: 5, 7, 8, 24, 9, 5, 25, 23)

THE EDUCATION SERVICE

The Education Service, along with Design and Press and
Public Relations, is part of the Public Services Department.
It was started in 1970 and replaced the Guide-Lecture
Service established in 1911. Its main role is twofold:
services for adults, and for schools and colleges. The adult
programme consists of daily gallery talks, Monday to
Saturday, lunchtime lectures, Tuesday to Saturday in the
200-seater Lecture· Theatre, and an afternoon film
programme, Tuesday to Friday. In addition there are talks
for specific groups (e.g. NADFAS), and study days on topics
ranging from Buddhism to the Crusades, and from
Prehistoric archaeology to modern Japanese art. For the
Open University we organise intensive day schools, and
there are usually evening lecture programmes for major
exhibitions. We have initiated and organised two very
popular 'touch' exhibitions that had special facilities for the
visually and physically handicapped, but were also open to

the general public. A third is being planned. (Attenborough 1985: 144-5, 22)

Peter Mann's very limited survey of one week's participants in adult museum events (June 1983) revealed that 45% of them were aged 55 and over, and that 36% of those attending more than one event were over 65. Three-quarters of the lecture audiences were UK residents, although many foreigners came to gallery talks and films. Only 19% of lecture audiences were first timers. Not surprisingly, over half of the attenders at events had attended events at other museums. Up to 200 may attend a Tuesday lecture on Egypt; large audiences have also turned up on snowy winter evenings to hear about Anglo-Saxon art, or at lunchtimes for lectures on Raphael, Troy, Tibet or the Parthenon (Mann 1986: 50-1).

Perhaps as many as 100,000 children and students in school and college groups visit the Museum each year. The service for schools and colleges ranges from one day courses for 80 primary school teachers preparing to use a BBC TV series on the Greeks, to study days for 100 or more sixth formers on Roman Britain, women in Ancient Greece, or German Expressionism. In addition to giving talks in galleries or with slides in the Lecture Theatre, the Education Service provides a free 'mail order service' of resources for teachers preparing visits, or pupils involved in project work, now an important part of GCSE courses. Five thousand children may pick up an 'Asterix' trail during the Christmas holidays, when Asterix films are being screened. Printed trails at the British Museum - as at the National Gallery - may suggest themes that link a sequence of rooms or cases (e.g. Chinese Animals and Monsters, or Hunt the Hieroglyphs) in such a way that children don't have to read labels, but look, think, speculate (Reeve, 1983) (BM Report 1981-84: Appendix 9).

An important part of our work is to test preconceptions about Celts, Vikings, 'eskimos', or Indian religion and art. Children and adults alike are conditioned by Hollywood, TV, children's comics, 'received opinion'. If we don't confront their preconceptions, then visitors will come to their own conclusions. One child on a well-organised secondary school visit recently reported on having seen a very early railway track in our 'Archaeology in Britain' exhibition. It is in fact a pre-historic pedestrian trackway from Somerset.

Our resources - videos, teachers' packs, as well as trails - also seek to motivate, to select and locate the most useful range of objects, and to develop greater confidence among our educational users. This is also a major function of our teacher-training programmes with the London University Institute of Education, and Goldsmiths' College etc. We need a system for trainee teachers, akin to the American 'internship' in museums, if teachers are to be more adept at using museums as a central part of their work. Not surprisingly, art and design teachers are more willing than many of their colleagues to 'deconstruct' the museum experience and to extract what they need: heads, jewellery, animals, friezes, colour, pattern, the human figure. A group of 15 year old girls from Peckham, making their own ceramic heads, selected from source material that included Assyrian heads, Boy George, the Buddha, Benin Bronzes and Ancient Egypt. The Museum helped their motivation enormously: the function of the visit was not to learn more about Africa or Buddhism, but they are at least now more familiar with non-European art (Dyson 1986:48-55). The success of museum projects like this has encouraged other teachers to use the British Museum in a more imaginative way.

One can look at the collections through the eyes of artists like Henry Moore, or Burne-Jones, and how the Museum inspired them (Moore 1981; Denvir 1984: 192). Michael Ayrton, (1971: 34) as a 12 year old visited the Print Room for the first time with his father. 'Drawing is a method of thinking (he wrote later) and I learnt to think that way in the British Museum Print Room.' (Ayrton 1971:34) The Print Room today can only cope with very small groups of students; there is no permanent display of prints and drawings. Major exhibitions in the Museum, travelling exhibitions, illustrated catalogues, slide packs (some of them produced by art teachers) and video can help make the national collections better known, but the problem of accessibility here is critical. The lack of space hinders the further development of a major educational resource in the Museum (Griffiths and Williams 1987), (BM Report 1981-84: Appendix 5).

USING THE COLLECTIONS

As previously noted the Museum was founded in 1753, after the purchase of Sir Hans Sloane's collections by public lottery. It was not set up on the basis of a former Royal collection, as in Paris or Madrid or Leningrad, and was not conceived as a national museum in the sense of being a 'Museum of Britain'. It gathered together the existing national collections of manuscripts, became the National Library, and national collections of 'natural and artificial productions'. The 1753 Act observed that:

> all arts and sciences have a connection with each other, and discoveries in natural philosophy, and other branches of speculative knowledge ... do and may ... give help and success to the most useful experiments and inventions; (26 George II, c. 22)

The ideal was an encyclopaedic one of Sciences and Arts together, in tune with Enlightenment thinking (Hampson 1968: 11, 86). Had this been achieved, the Museum would now have all the collections of the South Kensington museums under its wing, as well as the National Gallery and National Portrait Gallery.

Today the Museum is the national collection of antiquities, prints and drawings, ethnography, organised in nine departments. The books and manuscripts are now in the British Library, since 1973 a separate organisation, although much of it is housed in the Museum building, at least for the time being.

I shall now look in more detail at three aspects of the development and educational use of the collections: the Classical and British Collections, and the multi-cultural use of the Oriental and Ethnographic Collections.

The Classical collections

In the eighteenth and nineteenth centuries not only were the classically educated public to be edified by the heroic art of the Romans, and, increasingly, moved by the art of the Greeks. Artists too were to learn to draw the human form, according to Sir Joshua Reynolds' 'Discourses', by studying classical sculpture even before attending life class. The Ancients in his view had achieved perfection and so the Royal Academy (founded in 1768) like Reynolds himself, had a collection of casts. The Roman Collections of Reynolds' friend Townley can be seen again in the Museum basements, displayed in a way reminiscent of the 18th century Vatican galleries. Many paintings by Reynolds, Zoffany and West

show the influence of such classical sculpture: the stance of
many of Reynolds' male subjects, the costumes and props of
his ladies, the allusions to classical theatre, festivals and
deities. Reynolds' description of the proposed contents of
the Royal Academy library gives us a good idea of what an
18th or 19th century artist might look for in the classical
sculptures of the Museum:

> bas reliefs, vases, trophies, ornaments, dresses, ancient
> and modern customs and ceremonies, instruments of
> war and the arts, utensils of sacrifice, and all the other
> things useful to students in the arts. (Rodgers 1986:49)

During 1986 we collaborated with the Royal Academy
Education Department at the time of their major exhibition
on Reynolds. Sixth form students of art history, art and
design, and classics, looked at how the 18th century artist,
sculptor, architect, stage designer, landscape gardener used
and recreated the classical. We concentrated on the
Townley Collection, which is once again a favourite with art
students drawing in the galleries. Now that the 20th century
Modern Movement's reaction against the classical has
abated, architects and artists are returning to classical
source material in the Museum, but as one option - not as
the only 'correct' style. In looking at classical architecture,
we have not only substantial fragments of Greek temples
and tombs, but the Greek Revival Museum building itself,
and in Bloomsbury and Covent Garden classical buildings by
Inigo Jones and Hawksmoor, many twentieth century
classical buildings (such as Burnett's King Edward VII
Building for the Museum) and Terry Farrell's post-modernist
greenhouse in Covent Garden itself.

Although classics today is no longer an automatic
ingredient in the education of a ruling class, the classical
collections are increasingly used by the complete range of
the Education Service's customers. Classics in schools has
felt itself under threat since at least the Education Bill of
1902, at the time when the Classical Association was
founded. At that time 16 year olds in grammar or public
schools spent 65% of their time on the classics (Stray
1986:6). In the 1960s JACT and the Cambridge Latin and
Schools Classics Projects took the lead in reforming classics
teaching, in broadening its appeal by emphasising the social,
historical and archaeological background, and therefore
propelling many more students of classics and classical

studies towards the Museum.

Since 1908, in addition to the normal art historical arrangement of the classical collections, there has been a display on Greek and Roman life, most recently reorganised in the 1980s with school groups especially in mind. The cases are grouped into public and private themes, including women, gladiators, transport and the Greek drinking party. The panel texts for each case (available to teachers as a booklet on the room) are a good example of the Museum's House Style. Now that the emphasis in education is so much on individual or group learning, this Greek and Roman Life Room is one of the most intensively used in the whole Museum. For example, as a result of a BBC Schools TV series on the Greeks, watched by 25,000 schools, 15,000 top juniors visited the Museum.

The comments of the French scholar Reinach on the original display still apply today:

> If it is desirable that antiquity should be made accessible to the public at large, and if one wishes to arouse the interest and win the sympathy of non-specialists, then this is an exhibition which any major museum of antiquities ought to be proud to set up. You have only to witness the large numbers of people who visit the new gallery every Sunday and listen to what they have to say to see how readily antiquity can be brought to life. (Jenkins 1986:67)

Today we visit the ancient Mediterranean world on holiday, or as surrogate tourists in museums nearer home, or by watching a TV series like Michael Wood's In Search of the Trojan Wars. This series in 1985 resulted in enormous interest in educational events at the Museum. We ran several study days on the Trojan Wars, with the help of singers from Kent Opera and the Royal Opera House, focusing on their productions of Tippett's King Priam. An extraordinary emotional impact was made on very varied audiences of adults and sixth formers. It is essential to engage the emotions of students reading Virgil or Homer in the twentieth century, or looking at a Greek vase painting that depicts Priam being killed on his own altar, beaten about the head with the body of his grandson. We have also collaborated with Kent Opera in studying Nero, The Magic Flute and Dido and Aeneas, and with the English National Opera on Egyptian operas such as Aida and Philip Glass'

Akhnaten.

The British collections

Many twentieth-century visitors expect to see the 'history of Britain', but not until the mid-nineteenth century was the Museum almost forced into collecting early and medieval British history. Hitherto in antiquities it had concentrated particularly on classical art - Townley's Roman marbles, Hamilton's Greek vases, the Elgin Marbles.

The British, Medieval and Oriental collections begin to develop only with the appointment of Augustus Wollaston Franks in 1851. Under pressure from a donor and from a Royal Commission in 1849-50, the British Museum at last set aside a room for British and Medieval antiquities. Hawkins, the Keeper of Antiquities, was clearly not convinced. In response to a question from the 1860 Select Committee on the British Museum about 'Byzantine, Oriental, Mexican and Peruvian Antiquities stowed away in the basement' he replied: 'I do not think it any great loss that they are not better placed than they are,' (Wilson 1984:12).

Franks, as a Prehistorian and Medievalist, among other interests, was 'one of the very few professionals in the country'. He was the friend of great collectors and archaeologists, such as John Lubbock, banker, Chancellor of the Exchequer, friend of Darwin, much involved in the debate on Evolution, and a pioneer Prehistorian. Through this web of friendship, the Museum's collections grew. If the Trustees would not buy, then Franks bought himself, notably the Franks Casket, an eighth century decorated whalebone box from Northumbria, now a major exhibit in the Early Medieval Room (Wilson 1984:17, 30) (Caygill 1981: 41-44).

In Franks' day, display was usually not didactic but object-centred: the aim was to show as much as possible. The collections in Franks' department 'occupied 90 table cases and 31 upright cases - to say nothing of the numerous objects placed over cases, or on walls'. Even today some people such as the artist Paolozzi, recall this type of display with affection (Wilson 1984:19; Paolozzi 1985:24-28).

Today the British collections are to be found in a tightly restricted corner of the first floor, because so much of the Museum building had already been allocated to other departments by Franks' time. In the 1980s it is the British collections - rather than the Egyptian or Greek and Roman - that are growing rapidly as a result of current archaeology. Eight hundred years of Early Medieval Europe have as much room as four hundred years of Roman Britain, or early Cyprus: one room each. The Early Medieval Room shows how difficult it is to present a vast amount of material, some of it art historical, much of it archaeological, in a meaningful sequence, with adequate explanation, where the space is so restricted, and the display is therefore likely to intimidate the unprepared visitor.

Fortunately there has been a revolution in the way history is taught in schools, and the Sutton Hoo ship burial (on show in the Early Medieval Room) is part of that revolution. It is one of the examples of historical interpretation featured in the Schools Council History 13-16 Project. This puts the emphasis on skills, rather than on bodies of knowledge, and looks at the way historians and archaeologists reach conclusions about the past (Schools Council 1976).

Some earlier historians, such as the medievalist Tout in 1910, had already stressed that 'what was studied was in some ways less important than how it was studied, since the methods ... were transferable' (Richardson 1986:18). One of the defences today for history's place in the school curriculum, is that it helps develop critical life skills, the ability to assess and interpret evidence, whether a party political broadcast or an Anglo-Saxon ship burial. This 'skills approach' is ideal for tackling inevitably inadequate samples of past societies, as seen in archaeological and historical museums.

It is difficult to leave the Early Medieval Room still believing that 'The Dark Ages' were a regrettable lapse between Rome and the (Christian) 'Middle Ages' or that the Saxons and Vikings led a squalid, violent existence, unrelieved by culture. The major Viking exhibition at the British Museum in 1980 also opened many people's eyes to the intricacies of Viking art. Vikings are now firmly enshrined in the popular imagination, still often with horned helmets and a lack of moral scruples, but combined with some awareness of what historians and archaeologists have been saying for many years. It is impossible to say how far the exhibition itself contributed to this, given Magnus Magnusson's concurrent BBC TV series, and the growing public interest in the Coppergate excavations at York, culminating in the hugely successful, American-inspired 'Jorvik' experience.

Professionalism and general popular interest in archaeology have grown in parallel with the Museum. The oldest archaeological journal in the world was founded in London in 1770, and in the twentieth century Antiquity in 1927, Current Archaeology in 1967 and the glossy Popular Archaeology in 1979, for example (Musty 1986).

Archaeological societies flourish, as do evening classes. The Education Service and curatorial staff often lecture to such groups. There has been a growth of interest in archaeology in schools, fostered especially by the Council for British Archaeology, Sheffield and Southampton Universities, and now English Heritage. There is now a GCSE in archaeology, as well as A levels, and an increasing demand for places at university.

Apart from collecting medieval British archaeology, the 'Medieval and Later' Department also collects post-medieval decorative arts, like the Victoria and Albert Museum, but not on the same comprehensive scale. Its Modern Collection is a small study collection, part of the Museum's current policy to collect the contemporary. (Collins 1987) Other contemporary collections include Medals and Coins, British, American and German prints and drawings, oriental arts and, of course, ethnography. This has resulted in several popular exhibitions (BM Report 1981-84:10) (Griffiths and Carey 1980, 1984: Smith 1983, 1985).

THE MULTICULTURAL CURRICULUM IN THE 1980s

One of the priorities of the British Museum Education Service in the 1980s has been to develop a greater interest in the non-European world and multicultural Britain among the 'general' public, schools and colleges, and teachers in training. Despite the greater emphasis on multicultural education in many local education authority directives, in teacher training and education generally (notably the Swann Report, 1985), the most popular areas of the Museum with teachers are still Egypt, Greece and Rome.

Today our multicultural work concentrates on two main areas: the Oriental collections in the British Museum main building, and the Museum of Mankind, which is the ethnographic department of the Museum, but is now housed in a separate building in Burlington Gardens (behind the

Royal Academy).

Japan has recently been the easiest of our oriental collections to promote to schools, partly because Japan is perceived as being 'advanced' and 'European', unlike India which is often perceived as a Third World society. Japan's art, particularly prints, tends to be more familiar to art teachers than Indian art: one needs less background information before tackling a print of a nineteenth century Japanese street scene, or a view of Mount Fuji, than one does in looking at Buddhist or Hindu sculpture. Japan is also familiar to school children through motorbikes, the Sony Walkman, Samurai, martial arts and 'Monkey' films on TV. The popularisation of Japan's art in the 1980s has been greatly helped by a series of exhibitions - 'The Great Japan Exhibition' at the Royal Academy most notably. Exhibitions about the art of China and India have been more sporadic.

At the British Museum Japanese exhibitions have included 'Japanese Prints' (1980), 'Edo' (1982), 'The Japanese Print Since 1900 - Old Dreams and New Visions' (1983). For 'Edo' we organised with the Japan Information Centre (the Education section of the embassy) a series of day workshops for teachers and students, including lectures, films, handling, practical calligraphy and a Japanese lunch box. The Centre produces the very useful Japan Education Journal and organises work-shops all over the country.

For the 'Edo' exhibition 7,000 copies of our trail were picked up from the exhibition, or sent out in advance to teachers; many adults picked one up to help them go round the exhibition, and then put it back again. It is easy to under-estimate the need for learning materials for adults in museums: the glamorous, often heavy and expensive catalogue or exhibition book does not help the visitor to go round an exhibition. There is a need for a cheap exhibition guide, such as that provided by the Royal Academy for their exhibitions. One reason for the success of the 'Edo' exhibition was the clear way it was organised, with sections on 'Samurai', and 'food and drink'; as well as 'metalwork', 'lacquer ware' and the other kinds of categories often used by curators, which are sometimes determined by conservators. Because of a careful selection of objects, the visitor did not feel too overwhelmed (Smith and Harris 1982). For the public events programme for the exhibition, we included a season of Sunday afternoon showings of Japanese films about the Edo period, with help from the British Film Institute.

The British Museum

We are now waiting for the results of the public appeal in Japan and Britain for £5,000,000 for a new Japanese gallery and study centre in the Museum, which will enable us to offer Japan on a permanent basis rather than relying on temporary exhibitions, since at present little Japanese art is displayed. The Victoria and Albert Museum has just opened its own Toshiba Gallery of Japanese Art.

China, like Japan, has been the subject of a major Royal Academy exhibition; it has received a lot of specific media attention, notably The Heart of the Dragon series on Channel 4, and can be perceived as relevant to teaching about the modern as well as the ancient world. Despite this it does not have the prominence in schools or the public attention that it deserves. There are excellent teaching materials now on China, ancient and modern, produced by the ILEA, for the former Schools Council, and by commercial publishers. Marco Polo often figures in the type of syllabus where Europeans still 'discover' the rest of the world. Primary teachers are often loathe to branch out from the diet of ancient Egyptians (honorary Europeans), Romans, dinosaurs and Vikings; and the secondary school often concentrates only on Mao and modern China. At the Museum we have attempted to interest younger children in the holidays with our 'Chinese Animals and Monsters' trail. This worked very well as a specific promotion with publicity in the Press, on LBC's 'Kids Line', and in publicity to schools: children followed the trail's 'Tiger' symbol up the north stairs, from the north entrance to the Oriental gallery. Normally, however, children arrive at the main entrance, both as school parties and family groups, and seldom penetrate to the far end of the building. We constantly stress to teachers on courses that their life would be much easier in the less crowded oriental gallery, rather than doing battle yet again with the Mummy rooms, but this tactical argument - allied to the very good multicultural reasons for studying the Far East - seems to have had little effect. We return to the need for better initial and in-service teacher training, and the need to break the 'Catch 22' situation of primary teachers doing Egypt because they did Egypt themselves at primary school, and so on.

Our Chinese trail has been translated into Chinese, and an element of it on dragons was expanded into a special 'Dragons' trail for the temporary exhibition 'Chinese Ornament: the Lotus and the Dragon' (1984-85). The exhibition and the trail were used by multi-ethnic primary schools doing projects on the Chinese New Year. In redisplaying parts of the China gallery, dragons and phoenixes were given a bay to themselves, and this has made it much easier to develop the topic with children and the public. The adult response to the 'Chinese Ornament' exhibition was very interesting: adults were prepared to make a considerable effort to grasp the often complex ideas behind the exhibition and came back repeatedly to gallery talks and lectures, many of which were given by the curator responsible for the exhibition (Rawson 1984).

For the Festival of India in 1982 the Museum organised two exhibitions: 'Vasna - Inside an Indian Village' (at the Museum of Mankind, later shown at Leicester), and 'From Village to City in Ancient India' (Durrans and Knox 1982). Some schools managed to combine visits to both, but it was 'Vasna', with its reconstructed weaver's house, Hindu shrine and bullock cart that attracted them most. Early India - particularly the Indus valley culture - is one of the great early civilisations, with the earliest planned cities anywhere, at sites such as Mohenjo Daro. By contrast with ancient Egypt or Minoan Crete though, there is limited visual evidence, and no identifiable personalities. The cities themselves were built of mud brick and are badly eroded. The Indus valley script has still not been deciphered and is found on tiny seals that would anyway be unlikely to yield great secrets. There is little sculpture. Teachers in schools with Indian or Pakistani ethnic groups (most of the Indus valley sites are now in Pakistan), have tried to tackle early India, but it is tricky: the Museum has only two cases devoted to it, and the objects are small. To interest particularly young children during the Festival of India, and to try and break down teacher resistance to Indian art, we produced a children's trail, which introduced the Indus valley material, but concentrated mainly on the stories behind Hindu sculpture. The stories of Ganesa, Siva, Vishnu and the great goddess Durga can be told very successfully around the sculptures to small children or to adult groups. Durga is an especially useful antidote to the predominant machismo of most mythologies, where male gods do, and female gods merely embody beauty and wisdom.

On the whole, primary teachers and art teachers are still resistant to Indian art, and it is as part of the growing emphasis in secondary school religious education on world religions that this material is most used. ILEA's Ramayana Festival in Summer 1987, to which we are contributing, may arouse greater interest in the arts of Hinduism. India has, after all, received a great deal of attention on TV and in the cinema.

Each year we organise study days for sixth formers and teachers on the major world religions with the London University School of Oriental and African Studies' External Division: e.g. on 'Islamic Art and Design', a British Museum exhibition in 1983 (Rogers 1983). The exhibition trail 'Turbans and Tulips' was also available in Turkish, for Turkish educational groups, particularly in north and east London.

The Museum now has one of the world's finest collections of Islamic ceramics, particularly after the Godman bequest in 1983. This has become an attractive area of the Museum for art colleges, NADFAS groups and art teachers, and even with some maths teachers, interested in patterns and geometry. Teaching Islamic art at the British Museum will be greatly helped by the new Islamic Gallery (to open in 1988), and the major exhibition 'Süleyman the Magnificent' from Istanbul (Rogers and Ward 1988). The new Islamic Gallery will bring together all our major material in a treatment co-ordinated geographically and chronologically, and thus provide the context which is missing at present.

The interest generated in primary schools by the BBC TV Watch series Arabs and Islam (watched by over 20,000 schools) has tended to go more to the Victoria and Albert Museum, which has much larger objects, such as pulpits and tile friezes, in a substantial gallery space ideal for group work, or to the London Mosque in Regents Park (with which we have also collaborated on sixth form days). In 1987 we offered a course for primary teachers, looking both at our Islamic art and our Arab ethnography (some of which was displayed in the very popular 'Nomad and City' exhibition in 1976). We are also using Arab volunteers to talk to school groups and other volunteers to work with schools in a special handling room, at the Museum of Mankind. One of the main aims of these Arab events is to counteract stereotype and prejudice, which is especially evident in the popular press, and to get away from the often 'exotic' view of Arab culture that we have in the West.

The most ambitious of all our multicultural exhibitions and education programmes has been 'Buddhism: art and faith', a joint British Museum/British Library exhibition, for six months in 1985, attracting over 200,000 visitors, but, because of the teachers' industrial action, very few schools. The adult response - particularly to gallery talks in the exhibition - was on a scale normally seen here only for Egypt or the Parthenon. For the first few weeks the audience numbered between 70 and 100 people for each talk in the exhibition, and two of us had to give gallery talks in relays. One of the major problems for the public was the unfamiliarity of much of the material, and the sheer quantity of it: over 400 exhibits from India across to Japan, arranged partly geographically and partly around themes such as 'heaven and hell' and 'the transmission of the scriptures'. Normally the Education Service is closely involved now in the planning of exhibitions and new galleries, but on this occasion it proved difficult to have much impact on a large body of curators in two institutions faced with a daunting problem (Zwalf 1985).

Consumer research among young children and adults showed they did not respond to colourless stone Buddhas, or to faded or very complicated paintings, but to the brightly coloured 'cartoon-strips' of the Buddha's life, and the more glittery sculptures, often bejewelled gilt bronzes, especially from 19th century Burma. (For many of us Burmese art was one of the greatest revelations of this exhibition.) In the postcard pack, and the 12 minute exhibition video that we produced to send out to schools and colleges, we tended to concentrate on these more accessible images, and to project a story line. The Buddha is seen leaving the palace for the last time, having decided to renounce his life as a prince, and seek enlightenment; he pulls back the curtain to take a last look at his wife and son; the gods come down to muffle the hooves of his horse as he rides away. In a Burmese cosmography, brightly coloured elephants are seen admiring themselves in a lake, while elsewhere in the forest can be seen Disney-like deer and tigers. The postcard pack provided a highly selective introduction to the exhibition; teachers will be able to use it even when the exhibition is over, to counteract the often rather colourless and static impression of our permanent display on Buddhism, and the absence of manuscripts and books in the Museum's displays. (The British Library displays a small sample in the King's Library.)

In video and gallery talk we inevitably produced an alternative structure to that of the exhibition; we were trying to provide linking themes that were not overt in the exhibition organisation itself. We tried to develop the learning skills of the public, for example introducing them to basic iconography: the position of the Buddha's hands (often in the teaching position); the bump on the Buddha's head, which begins as a bun of hair to wrap a turban round, but is later stylised to form part of the head itself, as a symbol of his wisdom. The hair is shown rather like pasta shells, since texts describe how after shaving off his hair it did not grow again - the roots simply curling round to the right. We also tried to present the contrasting physical environment behind Himalayan Buddhism, as opposed to Sri Lankan or Japanese. Tibetan art often appears very turbulent and shows the need for savage-looking protector figures (derived from Indian art), which do not figure in the Buddhist art of the paddy-field and monsoon culture of other parts of Asia - such as Burma. Had the exhibition been devised as an educational project, these links could have been made overt: instead the aim clearly was to be as comprehensive as possible, without taking into account how people actually learn, and how easily they are intimidated by a barrage of unfamiliar images and facts (Reeve 1985).

Often many different types of public came to the same gallery talk, and one might in rapid succession be asked basic questions about what a bodhisattva or a stupa is followed by involved questions about theology by a practising Buddhist that I often could not answer. Fortunately other Buddhists in the audience often helped out, or I provided the name of a likely source of information.

Since the exhibition closed, the numbers attending gallery talks and lectures on Buddhist art and other oriental subjects have again shrunk to their previous proportions. Where has that public gone? Why do they appear for special events only?

The lessons we have learnt over the last 5 years are that we have to grasp every opportunity provided by a temporary exhibition, in order to promote oriental cultures or religions, and that it needs schools TV or on-going media interest to maintain public and school interest. Recent evidence suggests that there is still resistance to multicultural education among many teachers, particularly in areas with small ethnic populations (Nixon 1985: 7, 47 etc.). Museums can play a great role in answering this reluctance to use multicultural materials: Hindu art is after all no more remote from most people's experience than ancient Greek; we have to explain basic Christian stories to most children today, too. If the emphasis in history teaching is now really on skills rather than bodies of knowledge, then there is no reason not to include non-European material. In my experience, secondary school pupils can often become sick and tired of a Eurocentric diet of increasingly 'relevant' (i.e. modern) history.

The Museum of Mankind has also responded to the impact of BBC TV for primary schools, notably 'The North American Indians', and the series on Eskimos/Inuit. Thanks to the involvement of a curator in the preparation of this series, the Museum was able to put on a special display, and to produce The Eskimo Activity Book for children. The Education Service at the Museum of Mankind has also provided teachers' courses, teachers' packs, worksheets for the major exhibitions such as 'Asante' (West Africa), 'Hidden Peoples of the Amazon' and for the highly successful North American Indian exhibition, which was part of the American Festival in London in 1985. This featured demonstrations, for example by a totem pole carver, and was linked to a competition organised by American Express and The Observer. (The totem pole is now at the Horniman Museum.)

Major exhibitions at the Museum of Mankind often feature reconstructed environments - such as an Amazonian Maloca (long-house), or Asante king's palace. This often makes it much easier for children to relate to exhibitions there. We are therefore developing the education programme of the Museum of Mankind because of its great potential, with for example handling sessions linked to current topics - such as the Amazon or Inuit; holiday events have included body painting, the creation of several large murals, in addition to handling sessions, films and worksheets. The public programme now includes a regular Friday lecture, as well as the daily programme of film and video. We hope gradually to introduce some gallery talks for the general public. We will continue to collaborate wherever possible at the Museum of Mankind with outside organisations: these have included ILEA, the Commonwealth Institute and the Centre for Urban Educational Studies.

The Museum of Mankind clearly does not have the high public profile it deserves: its exhibitions do not fit easily, for example, into the art critic's brief. The lack of a large permanent display, and the range of exhibitions, present teachers with a considerable challenge. The ethnographic collections will eventually return to Bloomsbury, and their proximity to the permanent displays of oriental art at the north end of the building will create a much stronger focus on non-European art and society. Often unhelpful divisions between art and anthropology in collecting and display should also begin to break down as a result.

One event at the Museum of Mankind that has aroused considerable interest has been the controversial exhibition organised by the sculptor Eduardo Paolozzi, 'Lost Magic Kingdoms'. For this we have experimented with a gallery talk given by two of us with rather different attitudes to the exhibition and the way it uses ethnographic material. (The National Gallery and the Victoria and Albert Museum have also tried this 'dialogue' type of gallery talk with some success.) These talks and the exhibition itself have generated far more discussion than is usual from an English audience. (North Americans tend to be more immediately responsive in public and prepared to join in.) Art teachers and students have been extremely enthusiastic. Family groups have been invited to choose objects from the reserve collections and to recycle bric-a-brac, in order to make their own displays. A major function of a museum education service is to develop this 'enabling' function, encouraging visitors to feel more comfortable, making them more confident with unfamiliar material and mediating between the many different publics and what can seem like another of Illich's 'disabling professions' (Illich 1977).

Curators organise objects in very particular ways, and talk about them in a special language. The aim appears to be neutrality as a means to objectivity. Paolozzi on the other hand, has said 'This is what I like', 'This is what has influenced me', and 'This is how I think about art and culture'. He has initiated a debate, rather than trying to pin a culture down and recreate it through an inevitably limited sample of its material remains. Much of the anxiety and opposition engendered by multicultural education could be relieved if we accept that the best kind of education can be a debate between different perspectives.

> You are not here to teach a lesson, nor to tell all you know, nor to give all the answers. Your duty is not so much to tell as to ask; not so much to fix facts as to invite hypotheses. (ICOM 1956)

Whereas some anthropologists may feel that Paolozzi is just the latest European artist using the Third World as stimulus, it is also possible to see the exhibition as an antidote to the professional grammar of museum display

(Coombes and Lloyd 1986). This normally comprises: object/label/panel text/catalogue entry. The object 'represents' a lifestyle, a moment in time, a person, a cultural activity etc. The information provided is therefore potentially a source of education about another culture. Paolozzi, on the other hand, talks of the need to 'Kick the visitor up the backside'. There is no orthodox catalogue, most of the objects are unlabelled and are not arranged either in the familiar kinds of groupings - 'ivories', 'baskets' - nor in recreations seen elsewhere in the Museum of Mankind (Amazon rain forest, Asante palace). Instead Paolozzi has focused on concepts and themes; such as colonialism, heads, animals, the recycling of materials (Paolozzi 1985).

So while Paolozzi is on one level presenting his personal selection of source material (as some American curators overtly do, or artists have done in the National Gallery), he is also confronting - as most conventional museum exhibits do not - the criticisms of Professor Brian Lewis of the Open University:

> To the professional educator, the most conspicuous feature of conventional museum exhibitions is their communicative incompetence. The emphasis is plainly on the displaying of objects, rather than on the transmitting of ideas.
>
> Does any of this matter? If the general public is willing to settle for the kind of museum exhibition that provides little more than an enjoyable distraction from the problems of the moment, why should anyone attempt to do anything different? (Lewis 1980)

The Natural History Museum has taken the lead in meeting this challenge: its new galleries function primarily as a learning environment, rather than as a display of objects (Miles and Alt 1982; Alt and Griggs 1984). It is much more difficult for a collection of antiquities to do this, but less so for an ethnography museum dealing with living cultures. Future plans for the Museum of Mankind include exhibits on Bolivia, Indonesia, the Arctic, Mexico; an exhibition on Madagascar has recently opened, the result of recent field work in a society where African and Asian influences interact.

CONCLUSIONS

In 1981 a quarter of the adult British population visited a museum at least once.

The patterns of museum visiting are closely related to those for theatre, opera, dance and classical concerts. (Hooper-Greenhill 1988:217)

Much of the public now has greater opportunities for leisure, but this is not reflected in a wider social range visiting museums such as the British Museum.

The proportion of working class visitors was small - roughly one in ten, compared to two out of every three in the general population. (Mann 1986:5)

Organised groups in full-time education, mature part-time students, members of societies, highly motivated and well educated individuals are all increasingly well catered for by the Museum's Education Service. The unemployed, the less affluent and the less well educated are either not attracted to the Museum, or find the experience often problematic. It is unlikely that a national museum can attract a much wider public, either from further afield or more socially varied, just by putting on more popular exhibitions and events in London. A programme of what American museums term 'outreach' is much easier for a local museum to provide, with its specific community and local funding. The British Museum does send travelling exhibitions, and with increased resources could do a great deal more. Collaboration with the media can also help: the BBC 'QED' programme on Bogman (the prehistoric body found at Lindow Moss) was watched by about 8 million people.

Because of the varied nature of our publics, the Museum's Public Services Department, curators, and British Museum Publications will need to continue working closely together on interpretation and publications. There have been some considerable successes, such as 'The Ancient Olympic Games' in 1980, where the material was attractive, clearly displayed around a large reconstruction of Olympia, and drawing a wide social and age range to an exhibition on a topical and accessible subject that required little previous knowledge (Swaddling 1980). That was an unusual opportunity. As R.L. Gregory (1966:8) has observed:

> The seeing of objects involves many sources of
> information beyond those meeting the eye when we look
> at an object. It generally involves knowledge of the
> object derived from previous experience, and this
> experience is not limited to vision.

Throughout the arts - and particularly in museums -
there are tensions at present between the role of the
museum or arts body as part of an authoritative cultural
system, (handing on not only collections but values), and the
need to be more responsive to a wider public and their
interests and abilities (Pearson 1982:81, 99-100, 109).

E.H. Gombrich (a former British Museum trustee) has
summarised the central part of this tension from a
curatorial point of view:

> Our egalitarian age wants to take the awe out of the
> museum. ... Nobody should feel afraid to enter it, or for
> that matter be kept away by his inability to pay. But as
> far as I can see, the real psychological problem here is
> how to lift the burden of fear ... without also killing
> what for want of a better word I must still call respect.
> (Hibbard 1980:577)

In looking to the future we are having to adjust to a
society that has changed culturally, and to an education
system that is undergoing a major transformation. If the
school curriculum becomes more utilitarian then there will
be a growing role for museums as agencies of informal
cultural education.

BIBLIOGRAPHY

Alt, M. and Griggs, S., 1984, in Thompson, J.M.A. (ed.),
    Manual of Curatorship, London, Butterworth
Ames, M., 1985, 'De-schooling the Museum', in Museum 145,
    Paris, UNESCO
Attenborough, R., 1985, Arts and Disabled People, London,
    Bedford Square Press
Ayrton, M., 1971, 'Prints and Drawings', in Treasures of the
    British Museum, London, Collins
British Museum, Report of the Trustees for 1981-84,

London, BMP

Calouste Gulbenkian Foundation, 1982, The Arts in Schools, London, CGF

Caygill, M. 1981, The Story of the British Museum, London, BMP

Caygill, M. 1985, Treasures of the British Museum, London, BMP

Chadwick, A. 1980, The Role of the Museum and Art Gallery in Community Education, Nottingham University, Department of Adult Education

Collins, M. 1987, Towards Post-Modernism: Design since 1851, London, BMP

Cook, B.F. 1985, The Townley Marbles, London, BMP

Coombes, A. and Lloyd, J. 1986, 'Lost and Found at the Museum of Mankind' in Art History, Dec. 86, London, pp. 540-5

Denvir, B. 1984, The Early Nineteenth Century: Art, Design and Society 1789-1852, London, Longmans

Dyson, A. (ed.) 1986, Art History and Criticism in Schools, London, Association of Art Historians

First Division Association, 1987, A Stitch in Time, London, FDA

Francis, F. (ed.) 1971, Treasures of the British Museum, London, Thames and Hudson

Gregory, R.L. 1966, Eye and Brain, London, World University Library

Griffiths, A. and Carey, F. 1980, American Prints, 1879-1979, London, BMP

Griffiths, A. and Carey, F. 1984, The Print in Germany, 1880-1933, The Age of Expressionism, London, BMP

Griffiths, A. and Williams, R. 1987, The Department of Prints and Drawings in the British Museum - User's Guide, London, BMP

Hampson, N. 1968, The Enlightenment, London, Pelican

Haskell, F. 1976, Rediscoveries in Art, London, Phaidon

Haskell, F. and Penny, N. 1981, Taste and the Antique, New Haven, Yale University Press

Hibbard, H. 1980, The Metropolitan Museum of Art, New York, London, Faber and Faber

Hooper-Greenhill, E. 1988, in Lumley, B. (ed.) The Museum Time-Machine, London, Comedia/Routledge

ICOM, 1956, Museums and Teachers, Paris, ICOM

ICOM, 1984, Proceedings of the 13th General Conference 1983, Paris, ICOM

Illich, I. et al., 1977, Disabling Professions, London, Marian

Boyars

James, T.G.H. 1981, The British Museum and Ancient Egypt,
    London, BMP

Jenkins, I.D. 1986, 'Greek and Roman Life at the British
    Museum', in Museums Journal, September 1986

Lewis, B. 1980 'The Museum as an Educational Facility' in
    Museums Journal, December 1980, London, Museums
    Association

Lowenthal, D. 1985, The Past is a Foreign Country,
    Cambridge, Cambridge University Press

Mann, P. 1986, A Survey of Visitors to the British Museum
    (1982-83), Caygill and House (eds), London, British
    Museum Occasional Paper No. 64

Miles, R. and Alt, M. 1982, The Design of Educational
    Exhibits, London, George Allen and Unwin

Miller, E. 1973, That Noble Cabinet, A History of the British
    Museum, London, Andre Deutsch

Moore, H. 1981, Henry Moore at the British Museum,
    London, BMP

Musty, J. 1986, 'The Origins of the Archaeological
    Periodical', in Current Archaeology, 100, London

Newsom, B.Y. and Silver, A.Z. (eds.), 1978, The Art Museum
    as Educator, Berkeley, University of California Press

Nixon, J. 1985, Guide to Multicultural Education, Oxford,
    Basil Blackwell

Paolozzi, E. 1985, Lost Magic Kingdoms, London, BMP

Pearson, N. 1982, The State and the Visual Arts, Milton
    Keynes, Open University Press

Plumb, J.H. 1969, The Death of the Past, Harmondsworth,
    Penguin

Rawson, J. 1984, Chinese Ornament: the Lotus and the
    Dragon, London, BMP

Reeve, J. 1981, 'Education in Glass-Case Museums', in
    Journal of Education in Museums, 2, London, Group for
    Education in Museums

Reeve, J. 1983, 'Museum Materials for Children', in Hall, N.
    (ed.) Writing and Designing Interpretive Materials for
    Children, Manchester, Manchester Polytechnic

Reeve, J. 1985, 'Leading the Public to Nirvana? Interpreting
    "Buddhism: Art and Faith"', paper for the conference
    Making Exhibitions of Ourselves: the Representation of
    Other Cultures, at the British Museum 1986

Richardson, R.C. 1986, 'History Laboratory' in Times
    Educational Supplement 22 August 1986, p. 18

Rodgers, P. 1986, 'The Founders' Intention' in R.A., No. 13,

London, Royal Academy

Rogers, J.M. 1983, Islamic Art and Design 1500-1700, London, BMP

Rogers, J.M. and Ward, R.M. 1988, Süleyman the Magnificent, London, BMP

Said, Edward 1985, Orientalism, London, Peregrine

Schools Council History 13 to 16 Project, 1976, A New Look at History, The Mystery of the Empty Grave, Edinburgh, Holmes McDougall

Smith, L. and Harris, V. 1982, Japanese Decorative Arts from the 17th to the 19th Centuries, London, BMP

Smith, L. 1983, The Japanese Print Since 1900, London, BMP

Smith, L. 1985, Contemporary Japanese Prints, London, BMP

Stray, C. 1986, '1902 and All That' in JACT Review No. 5, London, JACT

Strong, R. 1977, The Victoria and Albert Museum Souvenir Guide, London, Thames and Hudson

Wilson, D-M. 1982, The British Museum and its Public, London, the Wynkyn de Worde Society

Wilson, D.M., 1984, The Forgotten Collector, London, Thames and Hudson

Wilson, D.M. 1984, 'The National Museums' in Thompson, J.M.A. (ed.), Manual of Curatorship, London, Butterworth

Wingfield Digby, 1974, Visitors to Three London Museums, London, HMSO

Zwalf, W. 1985, Buddhism: Art and Faith, London, BMP

Chapter Five

THE BBC

Neil Barnes and John Cain

INTRODUCTION

To understand the role of the BBC in cultural matters and
how this is affected by its relationship with the State, it is
first necessary to appreciate its constitutional position, its
size and the scale of the operation. The first part of this
chapter is devoted to this question, and, incidentally, tries
to clarify what 'the State' and 'cultural' seem to imply in
relation to the BBC.

In the second part some examples are given of the many
hundreds of ways in which the BBC contributes to the
cultural life of the country and how the output originates.
Thirdly we cite the example of educational broadcasting,
where the relationship between the BBC and the State is
more complex and misunderstood than it is in other areas of
output.

PART I THE BBC AS AN INSTITUTION

The Constitution

The Corporation has, as a broadcasting organisation, a
unique relationship with the State, interpreting that word
narrowly to imply Government. On a wider definition it is
difficult to speak about a relationship since some, at least,
would describe the BBC as part of the State, using the word
to describe all those instruments of the 'establishment'
which exercise profound influence and power in the country.
The dilemma of definition is clearly demonstrated by

pointing to the frequent assumptions made by foreigners, and some Britishers, that BBC employees are Civil Servants. They most certainly are not and they always deny it vigorously, yet that is a common perception. Why?

Part of the difficulty lies in the constitutional position of the BBC. It is a public corporation, set up under a Royal Charter, with 'Letters Patent under the Great Seal'. In this respect it is like many other UK bodies, for example the Corporation of the City of London and the Corporation of Trinity House. A corporation under British terminology is quite unlike an American corporation which is equivalent to a company in this country. A corporation in English law is a succession or collection of individuals treated as a single person and having 'a fictitious personality distinct from that of its members'. (1) There are, broadly, two kinds of corporation, a corporation 'sole' and a corporation 'aggregate', the monarch and bishops being examples of the former, the BBC an example of the latter. Corporations, which can only be created by the sovereign or by an Act of Parliament, are generally thought to exist in perpetuity but in the case of the BBC there is a clause in its Charter (No. 22) which provides for its 'Dissolution or Winding-up' either voluntarily or compulsorily. In these circumstances the property and assets of the Corporation, following the satisfying of debts and liabilities, 'shall be disposed of in accordance with the directions of Our Secretary of State'.

There are several references to 'Our Secretary of State' (short for 'Our Secretary of State in the Home Department') in the Charter and this raises the question of the BBC's relationship with Government. For example, the fourth paragraph makes it plain that it is this Minister who has 'represented for US' that 'it is expedient that the Corporation should be continued for the period ending on the thirty-first day of December One thousand nine hundred and ninety-six'. In other words it is the Government which determines the remaining length of life granted to the Corporation. Again it is the Home Secretary who grants the Licence and Agreement which fills in the detailed terms and conditions for operation not contained in the Charter, itself an enabling document. It is also to the Home Secretary that the BBC presents its Annual Report and he, in turn, presents it to Parliament. The members of the BBC, the Governors, who, in a strict sense, are the BBC, generally serve, on a part-time basis, for five years, unlike the members of the Board of Management who, under the Director-General, are responsible for the day to day running of the Corporation and have normal working contracts of varying lengths. The Governors are appointed by the Queen in Council (i.e. the Privy Council) but, in practice, this means by the Government. The twelve Governors have ultimate responsibility for all the BBC does including the appointment of senior staff, and stand both as the guardians of the public interest and of the interest of the Corporation. It has long been argued by some that this Janus-like role is an impossible one, but the fact is that the arrangement has worked, with little fundamental change since 1927 when the first Charter was granted. Before that time, from 1922, the BBC was a Company not a Corporation.

From the start the 'ethos' of the BBC was dominated by the first Director-General, John Reith, who had a strong conviction that broadcasting was concerned with the dissemination of information and education as well as entertainment. In wishing the programmes to be available to all those who paid a licence fee, the main source of income for the Corporation, and to their having high standards technically, morally and culturally, he was instrumental in refining and practising the original concept of 'public service broadcasting'. There was an undoubted paternalistic, even 'elitist', ring to this concept which set itself against competitive, market imperatives, but the quid pro quo was the creation of a rich, cultural cornucopia which became the envy of the world.

Government powers

The Licence and Agreement in particular reserves to the Home Secretary some specific powers other than those already mentioned. For example clause 13(4) in effect gives the Government the last word on matters in which its views and those of the Corporation might differ. In practice this has remained a reserve power except during the Second World War but history shows that day to day pressure from all governing parties, Right and Left, has been and is considerable. At the time of the Suez crisis in 1956 the then Prime Minister, Anthony Eden, came very near to issuing directives to the BBC but was persuaded this could be politically damaging.

In most of its programme activities, including those which might be described as cultural, the Corporation enjoys complete freedom but it is in the area of politics, current affairs, and more recently in matters of taste, that official displeasure is most often experienced.

There is a relatively small number of things which the BBC may not do. For example it cannot carry advertising, commercially sponsored programmes or broadcast subliminal messages. Neither can it express an editorial policy about matters of public controversy or public policy other than broadcasting policy. Equally there is a small number of tasks which the BBC is required to undertake, notably 'To broadcast an impartial account day by day, prepared by professional reporters, of the proceedings of the Houses of Parliament' (Licence Clause 13(2)). This required account is currently broadcast on radio and has been since 1945. In February 1988 Parliament agreed to an experiment in the televising of the House of Commons, the House of Lords having been televised since 1985. A further requirement is that the BBC broadcast official public information or emergency announcements whenever required to do so by a Minister of Her Majesty's Government (Clause 13(3) of Licence) but this has caused no difficulty. Quite separately the agreement under which Government (and Opposition) spokesmen are given facilities to broadcast ministerial statements and opposition replies is contained in an Aide-memoire first drawn up in 1947 and revised in 1969.

In addition to its Charter and Licence duties, the BBC, as a corporate citizen of the UK, is bound to observe the law of the land and, in particular, has to take special notice of the Representation of the People Act, and Race Relations Act, the Law of Defamation, the Official Secrets Act and law relating to contempt of court. It could be that, in the future, broadcasting will also come within the scope of the Obscene Publications Act.

Listeners and viewers who have complaints to make against the Corporation have a number of paths to choose from. These range from writing to producers, heads of departments, controllers, managing directors, the Director-General and Governors, to making application to the Broadcasting Complaints Commission, set up in 1981 to consider complaints of unfair treatment or invasion of privacy brought against the BBC and IBA, the governing body of Independent broadcasting. Ultimately, of course, the law can be invoked and this is happening increasingly as society in general becomes more litigious.

Impartiality

It is generally thought that the BBC, like the ITV companies (governed by the Broadcasting Act of 1981), is required to be impartial on controversial subjects and not offend against good taste and decency. In fact this is a self-imposed obligation contained in an Annex to the Licence and Agreement and follows a Resolution of the Board of Governors dated 8 January 1981. This in turn is based on a letter dated 13 June 1964 sent by the then Chairman of the BBC, Lord Normanbrook, to the then Postmaster-General, responsibility for broadcasting matters having been transferred from this Minister to the Home Secretary in 1974.

The concept of impartiality is a complex one and, in the BBC's view, centres on balance. However, there are two qualifications to be made. First, it is often not right or practical to seek balance within each individual programme. Second, it has never been BBC policy to impose balance on individual news bulletins, which must reflect the news accurately, without distortion for political purposes. During elections, of course, news coverage of electoral activity should be balanced. In general, fairness and balance must be sought over a reasonable period of time. These notions of impartiality, fairness and balance do not imply a god-like neutrality and detachment from the basic moral and constitutional assumptions on which the nation's life is founded. Thus the BBC is not neutral as between justice and injustice, freedom and slavery, tolerance and intolerance, truth and untruth. However, without a general policy of impartiality the BBC could not maintain its independent status.

The question of impartiality in cultural matters is a particularly interesting yet difficult one. For example, there have been numerous occasions in BBC history when charges have been made that individual plays are politically either too left-wing or too right-wing and there have even been accusations that serious television plays as a whole have a left-wing bias. Again, the documentary genre has often been associated with more radical thinking, which often means, simply, critical thinking, about society. These issues are part of a wider cultural debate about whether or not there is a general tendency for novelists, journalists, poets, playwrights to adopt particular social and political attitudes and thus whether the BBC is or is not in some sense the 'victim' of creative talent.

Finance and staff

The domestic services provided by the BBC are financed out of the revenue from the issue of broadcast receiving licences, which in 1986 amounted to just over £1,000 million. This is collected by the Post Office, which retains some of the money for administrative purposes. Some small further income comes from the sale of programmes, books and magazines. Thus the programme costs are largely met by those who view and listen and, in a sense, the public are 'shareholders'. By thus distancing itself from Government which could, after all, impose a straight grant, it is felt that BBC independence is maintained. Nevertheless the Government retains considerable financial power since it is Ministers who, from time to time, set the level of the licence. When this last happened in 1985 a novel and somewhat painful (to the BBC) precedent was set when it was decided that future adjustments to the licence would be linked to the Retail Price Index. This index rises at a rate below that of real costs in broadcasting, so, in effect, the BBC will be 'squeezed' in the future. Currently about 67% of the BBC's income goes to television, 25% to radio and the rest to capital costs and reserves.

The above funding arrangements pay for all domestic services (including Regional ones in Scotland, Wales and Northern Ireland). In contrast the programmes for overseas listeners to the External Services are funded by a direct Grant-in-Aid from the Treasury running in 1986/7 at about £99 million.

To operate the home services the BBC employs just over 24,000 staff whose salaries, along with those of a huge number of artists and speakers employed, account for a considerable proportion of the running costs. In other words broadcasting is very labour intensive. For example, in television, the biggest spender, 53% of its budget goes in production and other staff costs whilst a quarter goes in artists, speakers, royalties, copyright, recording and design materials. In order to meet the quality demanded today and bearing in mind the competitive impact of ITV and the film industry, television production costs are especially high in some 'cultural' areas. For example, drama can now cost up to £300,000 an hour to produce.

In radio the figures are, of course, much more modest but whilst the proportions of income spent on production, staff and artists are roughly the same, one can pick out one particularly valuable yet costly 'cultural' item, namely the seven orchestras and singing groups run by the BBC. These include the BBC Symphony and Philharmonia Orchestras, the Welsh and Scottish Symphony Orchestras and the BBC Singers, giving work to nearly 500 professional musicians and costing 3% of the £225 million radio budget.

The scale of the operation

With its one billion pound income the BBC offers two national television channels, four national radio channels, together with television and radio regional offerings from Scotland, Wales, Northern Ireland and five regions in England including over thirty Local Radio stations. There is also a teletext service called Ceefax. This very considerable output, amounting to roughly 10,000 hours of national television, nearly 4,000 hours of regional television, 30,000 hours of network radio, 24,000 hours of regional radio and 142,000 hours of local radio, in 1987 costs each licence payer 16p a day.

The BBC is often thought of as a highly centralised organisation and it is true that much power resides at Broadcasting House in central London from where BBC Radio and central administration operates. Nevertheless, it must be remembered that considerable production plant and devolved administrative power will be found in most of the larger cities of the UK with particular concentrations in west London, Glasgow, Cardiff, Belfast, Manchester, Birmingham and Bristol. Thus, apart from radio and television offered to local audiences, nearly one quarter of all UK network television and one eighth of all UK network radio programmes are originated in regional studios, although not all of this output reflects Regional as opposed to National interests. When considering cultural programming one must also remember, for example, the money and manpower put into Welsh and Gaelic output, (2) as well as the coverage of regional history, geography and daily life, which is heard regularly in all parts of the UK.

PART II CULTURAL OUTPUT AND HOW IT ORIGINATES

Definitions of cultural programming are bound to be imprecise and controversial but if, at the most general level, one includes within it current affairs, features and documentaries, news, educational programming, drama, religion and music then in terms of hours of output something like 42% of network television output and 47% of network radio output is, in some sense, cultural. In both cases those figures do not include children's programmes, sport and light entertainment. In the case of television films are excluded; the radio figure does not include popular music.

More specifically one can look at particular areas of clearly cultural output. For example, in television the BBC devotes about 7% of its hours of output to educational programmes for children and adults (excluding the many programmes which it makes for the Open University and which the University itself pays for). In 1985/6 BBC television transmitted thirteen major productions of classic plays apart from a huge range of serials, series and single plays. In radio there were, in the same year, sixty concerts in the Henry Wood Promenade series including several new works, some of them specially commissioned. Radio 4 broadcast plays by authors ranging from Ibsen to Rattigan and produced over 50 plays by first-time writers.

In the External Services which concentrate very much on news and current affairs, programmes about British culture, commerce and politics were broadcast in 1986/7 for a total of over 730 hours in 37 languages, including English, Britain now being fifth in the league table of world external broadcasters. In the World Service, which broadcasts in English, four great composers whose anniversaries fell during the year were honoured in 1985/6: Bach, Scarlatti, Handel and Schütz. The Transcription Service, which offers recorded BBC programmes to foreign broadcasters, in 1985-86 amongst many other things, distributed productions of works by Shakespeare and Noel Coward. In 1986/7 the World Service co-produced with Radio 4 the series Globe Theatre with plays by Shaw, Chekov, Miller, Molière and Pirandello.

A very sophisticated engineering operation is needed to transmit this massive amount of programming to the domestic and worldwide audiences. The BBC has always been the proud master of its own technology, often being in the forefront of developments. Some idea of the scale of this operation is indicated by the knowledge that, in the UK, apart from all the studios, cameras and recording machines, over 900 transmitters have to be maintained for domestic listening and viewing. The overseas operation depends on transmitters located in BBC sites as far apart as Singapore and Ascension Island.

Programmes originate in the BBC in an extremely varied and seemingly unstructured way. Broadly speaking the process is from the 'bottom-up' rather than 'top-down' which is not to say that every idea emerges from a producer or from the public. The producer, however, is an important seminal figure in every department and plays a particularly important role in those departments which can be said to have a significantly 'creative' output and where there is a reliance on ideas, imagination and performance.

Bill Nicholson, one of the BBC's most distinguished television producers, who amongst other things has produced the Everyman series and written the award-winning drama Shadowlands, has this to say about being creative within the public service broadcasting ethic:

> Everyone who works for the BBC knows that they are paid by the public, and work for the public. They know that the BBC does not exist to make money, but to spend it. This structural relationship between staff and general public has a thousand effects on the process of the work itself. We do not feel justified in pursuing entirely private obsessions. Nor do we feel compelled to maximise every audience for every programme. Compare the feelings of members of staff working for a commercial television company. They know that when all is said and done they are taking money from the viewers to give it to profit-making companies. We take money from our viewers to give it back to them as programmes.

> We who work for the BBC do not like to think of it as an instrument of state culture: but so it is. Defensive of our independence, yet proud to be servants of the public; freed from commercial pressures, yet eager for popularity; bureaucratic and anarchic; monolithic, and as tribally fragmented as the Lebanon; suddenly revolutionary and suddenly chicken-hearted; it's a very curious thing indeed, but it works.

Apart from the advantages of working within the public service ethic Nicholson attributes BBC creativity to the factors of size, the possibility of internal mobility between parts of the organisation, peer group competition and what he calls the no-profit ethic. Most BBC producers would probably agree, despite what some see as a cumbersome bureaucracy, the system ensures that first things come first, i.e. programmes, and that the BBC remains popular with the public, if not always with the State, because it produces high quality programmes more efficiently than anyone else. It does this, moreover, without constantly compromising cultural standards. It is well to remember, for example, that no broadcasting organisation in the world supports music to the extent the BBC does (including such concerts as the Proms), and that serious radio and television drama, still thriving in the BBC, has virtually disappeared worldwide from commercial systems.

Producers are grouped into departments of varying size each having a Head, who is responsible to the Controller above him. It is to Channel or Network Controllers (Controllers of BBC1, BBC2 and Radios 1-4) that most Heads submit their proposed programmes and from whom they obtain the necessary cash and facilities. Bids for these essential resources are made at regular 'offers' meetings and the competition is intense. The Network Controller will want to be convinced that the product on offer, which might be a simple single programme or an expensive series, is likely to bring credit to his Network in terms of prestige or a large audience or as part of a well-loved regular commitment. Similar structures exist in the National Regions of Scotland, Wales and Northern Ireland and in the five English Regions, which enjoy considerable, but sometimes, in their eyes, insufficient, autonomy. A recent fundamental reorganisation has provided the Regions with their own Managing Director who sits on the Board of Management.

The plans for new material come from numerous sources ranging from embryonic ideas planted by members of the public, to grand schemes submitted by creative writers and artists. Creative ideas rarely come from committees but they can act as useful 'sounding boards'. The BBC has over 50 Advisory Groups including those which specialise in music, religion, education and science.

Generally, the approach to programming is pluralistic and liberal with much creative freedom given to producers, who are judged on results. Difficulties or problems, when they occur, are 'referred up' for discussion and decision but recently there has been a move to strengthen local responsibility exercised by editors and heads and to minimise the 'buck passing' features of 'referring up'. The BBC, historically, has been and remains an organisation which makes its more severe judgements retrospectively, believing that very tight controls at the ideas and planning stages of new projects, particularly when they involve the imagination, will stifle creativity. The BBC was described by the Annan Committee in 1977 as 'arguably the single most important cultural organisation in the nation' and as 'a great patron of the arts'. Its cultural influence has been felt most obviously, perhaps, in music and drama but there are few broadcasting genres in which it has not been a pioneer. The cultural influences can, however, be more subtle and pervasive than bringing more music and more drama to more people. It is arguable that BBC broadcasters, over the last 60 years, have had a profound effect on speech habits, on the clothes we wear and the furniture we use, on the way we spend our leisure time and on our attitudes to nature, animals, old people and concepts such as charity and self-improvement.

It is inevitable that the BBC's contribution to the nation's culture focuses on its broadcasts but it would be misleading to assume the matter rests there. BBC Enterprises not only publishes the widely known Radio Times, which has constantly been a magazine best seller, and has, since 1929, offered the public one of the best intellectual weeklies, The Listener, (3) but is also one of the biggest book publishers in the UK. The range of subjects is vast, from cookery to philosophy, natural history to politics and many of these books reach the best selling lists.

PART III EDUCATIONAL BROADCASTING

BBC Education, although it is not typical of the BBC production output as a whole, (what is?), and receives only about 4% of the money spent on programmes, has a direct relevance to the theme of this book. This justifies special attention to its operation, particularly with regard to its broadcasts to schools, since much of the UK education system is of direct concern to central and/or local government. The BBC needs to walk the fine line between, on the one hand, being seen to be an agent of central government educational policy, and on the other, within the tradition of BBC editorial independence, being seen not to be responsible when deciding which educational priorities to pursue and approaches to adopt. In the creation of its broadcasts designed for use in schools and in some major national educational projects at the further or adult education level, the BBC is therefore very closely involved in matters which are also of direct concern to the State.

Visiting educators from overseas having heard about BBC broadcasts to schools and asking to see something of what goes on behind the scenes at Broadcasting House and Television Centre, often arrive with the assumption that the BBC is a State run organisation, and that the BBC's provision of educational programmes for schools is simply a means by which the Ministry/Department of Education distributes its centralised and officially sanctioned wares. This is frequently what happens in other countries in Europe and elsewhere, but it has never been the case in the UK. It is a remarkable aspect of the tradition of public service broadcasting in the United Kingdom that this is so. How has the BBC managed to be true in this area to its own traditions of independence while at the same time creating an output which is acceptable to both national and local government agencies and attractive to teachers and students?

Broadcasting designed to serve specifically educational purposes is almost as old as the BBC itself. The first BBC Director of Education was appointed by John Reith in 1924, when the letters BBC stood for the British Broadcasting Company.

The initiative in setting up a service of radio programmes for schools (and there were also adult education series) was part of Reith's vision of the proper role of a public service broadcasting system. It was certainly not the result of any outside demands from educationalists or pressure from the government. Sir Henry Richards, of the Board of Education (later the DES), writing in 1947, said

Teachers and administrators, local and central, were pardonably hesitant as to the possibilities of this new medium, and I well remember in the early days from 1924 to 1929 the sceptical though benevolent neutrality of my colleagues and myself of the Board of Education.'

These first few years of broadcasting to schools were by no means a resounding success and once the sheer novelty of radio had worn off, the weaknesses of the BBC's own approach to schools became more and more evident. As a result, teachers were brought in, for the first time, as active advisers and participants in programme making. And, most significantly, in 1929, the BBC itself set up the Central Council for School Broadcasting as a means 'to secure continuous contact between the BBC on the one hand and, on the other, the Board of Education, the Local Education Authorities and the whole body of teachers.' This Central Council, a body representing all aspects of education in schools, was not simply an advisory body, it had mandatory powers to prevent the BBC from broadcasting, to schools, programmes or series it felt to be inappropriate. With its array of Programme Sub-Committees this was the direct forebear of what in 1947 became the School Broadcasting Council for the UK (SBC) and in 1987, the Educational Broadcasting Council. The EBC still is today the body which stands sponsor for all programmes made by the BBC for use in schools and colleges.

The creation of the Central Council in 1929 can be seen to mark the point at which the BBC School broadcasting departments (a television service for schools started in 1957) committed themselves fully to contributing to the formal education system of 5-16 year olds in the United Kingdom.

Kenneth Fawdry, the Head of the School Television Department, wrote in 1973,

> The creation of this Council, involving the abrogation by the BBC of a small piece of its cherished independence, was judicious. It has helped to protect the BBC from public controversy in an area where this would doubtfully have had any constructive effects. ...
>
> Councils of this sort have to embody the idea of a representative democracy. They must also operate in a way which will command the respect of those whose work is affected by their decisions: in this case, the BBC producers. The double obligation was neatly met by making the Council itself predominantly a body of representative members appointed by educational organisations; and creating Programme Committees, through which the Council chiefly worked, composed of

men and women chosen for the contribution they could make as individuals working at the educational coalface. Thus the Council, while rarely exercising its mandatory powers except in a formal sense, could stand as the symbol of education's concern with broadcasting, and broadcasting's with education; while its committees could bring their personal experience to bear on the job of determining priorities, and hoist the red flag if they saw a serious danger of programme plans being 'unrealistic'.

The effectiveness of this relationship between the BBC and the Councils has varied over the years in the light of circumstances. The role of the Councils' own staff of Education Officers, originally independent watchdogs, now simply members of the staff of BBC Education, has changed remarkably over the past forty years. The extent to which lay members of the Programme Committees have been involved in the detailed planning of series or of programmes, has diminished. But in Kenneth Fawdry's view, the Programme Committees 'bear witness to the educational world that the basis on which programmes are devised and prepared is educationally valid.' And of the Council he believed that it had been successful at operating as a pressure group on the BBC on behalf of schools. It had been, he felt, less effective as a pressure group on the educational world on behalf of the BBC's contribution to schools.

Whatever the precise nature of the relationship between successive Councils and the BBC School Broadcasting departments during the nearly sixty years of their co-existence, public (licence fee) money has been spent by the BBC annually in making a regular and substantial broadcast provision for teachers at all levels and designed to be incorporated by them into the daily pattern of their classroom work. The only formal and accountable link between the BBC providers of this material and the receiving teachers has been the sequence of educational broadcasting councils.

The working of a system such as the relationship between the BBC and its School Broadcasting Councils can perhaps best be seen in operation when matters of high controversy are involved. Such was the situation in respect of the provision by the BBC, in the early 1970s, of sex education for primary school children. Those who sought to criticise the decision to make and broadcast these radio and television programmes, turned their annoyance onto the BBC. This was misplaced since it was the SBC's Primary Programme Committee which in 1967 had taken the initiative by asking the BBC to carry out an enquiry into current practice in primary schools as a preliminary step before deciding whether broadcasting might be an appropriate source of help for teachers. These preliminary enquiries encouraged the Committee to ask the BBC Radio and Television Department to make pilot programmes designed for eight and nine year olds. Education Officers held a large number of discussions and briefing meetings with teachers and LEA officials throughout the United Kingdom, in advance of the first transmission in 1970. The way in which the broadcast series were received and how they were used was then the subject of a detailed evaluative study submitted to the Programme Committee and the full Council. This is one example of many where the BBC, either with the initiative of the School Broadcasting Council or with their wholehearted support and encouragement has taken on the role of an initiator of the provision of a new and significant approach to educational needs.

And it is not only in the area of school based initiative that BBC Education in the past two decades has played a key role in new educational developments, thereby raising issues of national policy.

The mid-1970s saw the BBC Continuing Education Departments - radio and television - playing a major initiating role in the Adult Literacy Campaign of 1975-8. Its own field force of Education Officers had alerted the Departments to the growing awareness of a need to combat adult illiteracy and the advisory committees and Council endorsed this and the proposed BBC strategy to produce a range of series as part of a wider national campaign.

Though other agencies had pioneered the idea of a national scheme, it was undoubtedly the case that from the time of its involvement, BBC Education became the pace-setting agency, galvanising Local Education Authorities and others into becoming involved, designing the now universally recognised adult literacy symbol, setting up a national literacy telephone referral agency (still in existence in a much expanded form) and finally, as a result, prompting the DES into putting up £3 million over three years to help support local adult literacy schemes. Though it was by no means the BBC's own Adult Literacy Campaign, nevertheless the BBC provided the mainspring for it, while

Central Government, though giving general approval and encouragement, did not, until late in the day, take any real positive action.

What characterised these BBC projects and others, was that they were initiated as a result of the findings of internal research and/or of the advice or prompting of the BBC Educational advisory committees. And each project was financed, at least as far as the BBC's own activities were concerned, solely from its licence fee income. Furthermore, the BBC, having decided to act, then sought collaborative partners to play complementary roles in an overall scheme. The BBC was not the agent of someone else's campaign, however welcome official blessing, frequently given, might be.

But in recent years the nature of Central Government's role in all forms of education and training has been changing and this has increasingly affected the relationships with BBC Education. There has been a move to greater involvement coming not only by the DES but also by the Manpower Services Commission, the Department of Trade and Industry, the Department of Health and Social Security and others. The MSC, DTI and DHSS have each in their own ways 'trespassed' into the fields of education and training in the past decade and have been able to support their initiatives with often substantial direct funding, something the DES has traditionally not been able to do.

BBC Education has always welcomed opportunities in its adult education output to work alongside agencies which have shared educational aims - the adult literacy campaign was a case in point - provided that any extra funds were not required to be put into funding any of the broadcasts themselves; to enable the BBC to retain its editorial independence. So the willingness of Government agencies to join in such collaborative educational projects was enthusiastically welcomed when it began slowly to happen in the mid-1970s.

In the area of health education for example, the DHSS has channelled its funding through the Health Education Council (now the Health Education Authority). Health education has long been a specific priority for the BBC Continuing Education Departments but it was only in the mid-1970s that the beginning of a close collaboration was established between the BBC and the HEC (similar close links were established with SHEG, the Scottish Health Education Group). A sequence of joint projects have been undertaken, with BBC Education providing the programmes and the HEC funding the support literature, and carrying out the evaluation. Topics such as advice for childminders, help for those wanting to stop smoking, information about the dangers of excess alcohol consumption, routines of healthy living, child accident prevention, road safety, basic resuscitation techniques, each of these had formed the basis for one or more joint BBC/HEC projects in the past ten years. In many cases the topics have been non-contentiously educational; in others, particularly in the areas of smoking and drinking habits, the question of what is properly educational and what possibly propagandist has exercised the broadcasters' minds. How far it is appropriate to go down the road of collaboration with quangos is a question which must constantly be borne in mind. The most recent and most extensive area of collaboration between the DHSS and BBC - not just the educational departments in this case - has been the AIDS campaign which started in 1987.

This has been public education via the media on a grand scale, with the Government as such taking the initiative in contacting and involving all the broadcasting organisations, and massively supporting the campaign financially in the first six months.

Another topic area of increasing collaboration between BBC Educational broadcasters and Government departments is that of the provision of in-service education for teachers. In 1972, when the school leaving age was raised to 16, BBC Education, urged on by its advisory councils, involved itself, using entirely its own resources, in a major year-long sequence of radio and television series and accompanying publications designed to give teachers insight into the current approaches, then being adopted in the education of the older, less able and less motivated pupils. 'ROSLA and After' as the BBC project was known, was preceded by a major round of briefing meetings throughout England and Wales in an effort to encourage the constructive use of the materials by teachers and administrators meeting in viewing groups (the age of the video player had not then arrived).

The eventual success of this exercise was reflected in the comments of the Russell Report on adult education (1973) which referred to 'ROSLA and After' as a 'massive operation ... demonstrating the power of educational broadcasting to bring about a change of climate ...'. Yet the whole project had no official backing from the DES, though they were kept in touch with developments.

BBC Education in 1987 is once again involved in a major provision of in-service education for teachers. The clear need for extra support and encouragement of teachers of maths and science had been apparent for some years but had clearly now become an urgent national educational priority. It was a matter of concern not simply to the DES, but now also, because of the changed nature of the politics of education, to the DTI and the MSC.

An approach from BBC Education in 1986 to each of these agencies was not simply to gain support for what was being proposed, but also to seek their active financial backing. (The DES has recently altered the scope of the Educational Support Grant system and was, for the first time, effectively able to fund educational projects directly.)

The DES, DTI and MSC proved to be very interested in collaborating on a venture with the BBC which will result in a sequence of television series being transmitted in 1988, designed to provide up to date professional information and support for science and maths teachers and others involved in TVEI courses. The project represents a watershed, the BBC Board of Governors have approved that funding from these three Governmental agencies should be spent on making the television programmes themselves, though with safeguards for the continued editorial independence of the production teams built in. The justification for this change rested on the urgent nature of the national need coupled with the fact that the programmes were over and above the remit of the School Television Department. It is also the case that the decision occurred at a time when the question of the acceptance of outside funding, particularly in the form of sponsorship, was a matter of general debate, in the light of the pressures on the BBC finances.

The essential elements of the independent tradition of BBC broadcasts to schools nevertheless continue with an annual assessment of needs and priorities across the curriculum involving the active participation of the Educational Broadcasting Council and its programme committees. In this way, teachers receive from the BBC resource material to match their various classroom needs. In an age when each LEA was the arbiter of what its schools taught and the range of curricula was wide, the BBC needed to aim to appeal to the broadest range. Now with a standard national curriculum about to be imposed on all England and Wales, BBC Education will clearly want to be fully involved in contributing material central to the core curriculum while at the same time continuing to provide in significant quantities what it does uniquely well, a range of documentary and drama to contribute to the cultural, personal and social skills of the rising generation.

NOTES

1.   Jowitt's Dictionary of English Law (2nd edn., 1977).

2.   S4C (Sianel Pedwar Cymru or the Welsh Fourth Channel Authority) is an independent authority set up by Parliament to provide television programmes in Welsh. It is funded from subscriptions paid by ITV companies but the BBC provides several hundred hours of programmes per year without charge.

3.   Now jointly published with ITV.

Chapter Six

THE CIVIC TRUST AND AMENITY SOCIETIES

Ray Banks

FOREWORD

Voluntary societies of all kinds have played and continue to play a very important part in the way our country grows, develops and changes. Sometimes possibly not entirely free from arrogance or bigotry, they have nevertheless been able to exercise a steadying and moderating influence on Government and Local Authority thinking and to curb some of their at times excessive zeal for wholesale change. Their positive influence has also been considerable.

This is a vast subject and necessarily I shall tell the story as I see it. In large part it is a 'case history' of one Society, the Nottingham Civic Society, of which I have the honour and responsibility to be the Secretary. Any views expressed are mine and not necessarily theirs, though I hope they would agree with much that I have written.

I have had access to the voluminous records of the Society and my greatest problem has been that of selection. I have had to leave out so many things. What I have put in is therefore illustrative and not comprehensive. Perhaps some day a definitive history of the Society will be written as it deserves to be.

I set out with the intention of not mentioning individuals by name, but I soon concluded that it was appropriate to do so in certain cases. This means that there are those who have not been named and for this I apologise. Certainly it does not imply that I - or the Society - regard them any the less highly for their work.

The emergence and growth of the amenity society movement as we know it is very much a phenomenon of the second half of the present century. A few Societies are older than this, for instance the Birmingham Civic Society, which was founded in 1918, and of course there are others. Indeed we know that there was a Civic Society in existence in Nottingham in the 1920s, but none of its records appear to have survived. We know that, in 1926, it sponsored the publication of the well-known collection of T.W. Hammond drawings, 'Nottingham Past and Present'. If there is anyone reading this who can provide any information on that Society, I should be very pleased to hear from them.

The vast majority of such Societies were born in the 1960s and later. They owe their birth and continued existence to a change in public attitudes to planning and public participation which grew up when the euphoria of the years immediately following the war had subsided.

In the period just before the end of the war in Europe, we, as a Nation and locally, began to think about what we wanted our post-war cities to look like. The wholesale devastation of many of our cities had left the way clear for a new approach to urban planning. The greater the devastation, the clearer this approach could be. So the great cities - London, Plymouth, Hull, Coventry and many others - enlisted the great names of the planning world to prepare comprehensive new plans based on the best current ideas of urban planning. Cities not so widely affected by the bombing, such as Nottingham, also began to dream. Rightly or wrongly the impression is given that cost was a secondary consideration in many of these plans. Wholesale clearance and redevelopment was the order of the day and this led to the obliteration of much that was good and was capable of salvage.

The stirring of a new attitude was marked by the foundation of the Civic Trust in 1957. Its founder was Duncan Sandys (later to become Lord Duncan-Sandys), the then Minister of Housing and Local Government. It was formed as an independent body whose objects were summarised at its launch as being

- to encourage high quality in architecture and planning
- to preserve buildings of artistic distinction or historic interest
- to protect the beauties of the countryside
- to eliminate and prevent ugliness, whether from bad

design or neglect
- to stimulate public interest and inspire a sense of civic
  pride

This was an extremely wide remit to improve the urban
and rural scene in every way possible. The Trust was largely
financed by donations under covenant from leading business
and industrial concerns and it continues to operate as an
independent charity drawing its funds from voluntary
sources. It is not an 'official' body funded by Government,
though it gets Government support for some of its
activities.

One of the first projects initiated by the Civic Trust
was what became known nationwide as the Magdalen Street
experiment. Magdalen Street, Norwich, was a fairly typical
urban street and, in common with so many other shopping
streets all over the country, had an uninviting and uncared-
for look about it. The character of the street as a whole and
the personality of individual buildings had become
submerged in a jumble of discordant shopfronts, a clutter of
advertisements and traffic signs and a network of overhead
wires. Perhaps worst of all, there was a depressing drabness
due to the neglect of colour. The aim of the scheme was to
demonstrate how cheerfulness, dignity and a sense of unity
could be achieved at comparatively little cost, provided that
everyone would work together. It showed just how much
could be done by attention to harmony of colour and decor
between buildings in a street and how great was the scope
for improvement of shop-front appearance by attention to
the detailing of fascias and design of lettering. It inspired
local authorities all over the country to go out and do
likewise. The degree of success varied greatly. I was at that
time the Chairman of the Planning Committee of the
Beeston and Stapleford Urban District Council and we set
about applying these ideas to the High Road at Beeston. We
enlisted the advice of a well-known local architect and
worked very hard to persuade local shopkeepers to co-
operate in a co-ordinated plan of redecoration for their
premises. Our efforts met with only limited success, I fear.
We had to convince small businessmen that it was a good
thing to spend money which they often felt they could ill-
afford on work with no readily quantifiable benefit to them
in cash terms. Many of them were uneasy, too, about the
Council's long-term plans and their policies involving
changes in the shopping centre of Beeston. (An uneasiness

which still exists, incidentally). It also became obvious that even if improvements were achieved, they needed to be maintained over the months and the years. All the good work could so easily be negated, too, by a change of ownership or tenancy. We were dealing with a multitude of small businesses, some of which were prospering, some were not. Some were thinking of expanding, or of major alterations to their premises. Others were only facing the prospect of selling out. A town centre is never static - it is ever changing. This is a fact of life and has a major influence on the success or failure of any attempt at a 'uniform' approach to environmental improvements of any kind. In the housing field, the same lesson is very obvious.

We all learned a lot from the experiment - not least about human nature! - but we also came to realise, I think, that this was only one facet of a very much wider picture.

When the Civic Trust was formed in 1957, one of its main aims was the creation of a network of voluntary organisations committed to the protection and improvement of the environment. Since then, the number of societies listed on its national register has risen from fewer than 200 to over 1,000. The Trust has also promoted the development of federations of amenity societies, usually on a county basis. These now number over 40. Inclusion on the Trust's register implies recognition of a society as an active and responsible environmental pressure-group for the area concerned. Individual societies maintain their complete independence: they are not 'affiliated' to the Trust.

There are independent, financially self-supporting Associate Trusts in North West England (founded 1961), in Wales (founded 1964), in the North East (founded 1965) and in Scotland (founded 1967).

The Trust runs a valued service of information and advice to registered societies. It makes awards annually for good development of all kinds, publishes reports and holds conferences on current environmental issues. It responds to Government consultation documents, is represented on Government and other national committees, encourages the formation of building and preservation trusts, administers the Architectural Heritage Fund and the Heritage Education Group and maintains a library and collections of slides and photographs.

It is worth mentioning at this point the present 'Time for Design' experiment, in which Nottingham is one of six diverse local authorities chosen by the Department of the

Environment to participate. This very much carries on the tradition which was started by the Civic Trust. It is backed by the Royal Institute of British Architects, the Royal Town Planning Institute, and the National Housing and Town Planning Council. Broadly, its object is to encourage architects, planners, builders, local authorities, voluntary bodies and the general public to work together to improve the quality of the built environment. The Nottingham City Council has issued a series of design booklets, <u>A Design Guide for Shops and Shopfronts</u>, <u>A Code of Practice for Home Improvements</u> and <u>A Design Guide for Extending Your Home</u>. The Nottingham Civic Society has co-operated in the production of these booklets and in other ways. We have a seat on the 'Time for Design' co-ordinating committee. The experiment very much embodies the importance of a gentle, persistent, persuasive approach to the improvement of the environment, with which there is, I believe, a very considerable sympathy nowadays amongst the general public. It can be far more effective than the strident attack of some pressure groups, who shall be nameless!

A few years ago the Nottingham Civic Society instituted an award scheme for outstanding works affecting the environment - not only new buildings, but conversions, restorations and extensions. We present a Certificate of Commendation to the Architect and to his client. If outstanding or unusual skill and workmanship is involved, we present an additional Certificate to those who carried out the actual work.

Of course, it is easy to be dismissive of the attitudes of the immediate post-war years. With the ending of the destruction and devastation caused by the war, the time was ripe for radical approaches. The desire to sweep away the obsolete and derelict areas and rebuild on a grand new scale was uppermost. And we were very confident that it could be done. Even the concept of high-rise housing, which is now so much execrated and which went so tragically wrong for so many reasons, was born of a perfectly valid proposition. The idea of point-blocks, serviced by lifts and rubbish disposal facilities and having their own local shopping, public houses, health and social services and community provision and set in open landscape had a great deal to commend it. Indeed it does work in many other countries. I do not recollect any volume of dissent from amenity societies or the general public. Who could, at that time, have forecast the rise of anarchy and vandalism which had a great part in turning the dream sour? The lifts so often put out of action or polluted, the interference with rubbish disposal, the opportunities for violent crime, all of which made the tenants' lives a misery. The intricate and convoluted design of low-rise estates also, intended by architects to produce an attractive and varied living space, in fact encouraged crime and damage and made policing a nightmare. I think there is a cautionary message here for all amenity societies, Beware of backing the wrong horse!

Architectural fashions come and go. Unfortunately, converted into brick and stone, those fashions are all too permanent! We are not dealing with an art form, such as a piece of way-out, ultra-modern music, designed purely for the intellectual enjoyment of the cognoscenti. Architecture is part of our daily life - we cannot avoid it or close our eyes to it. We should not too readily mistrust our natural reactions to a proposed scheme. If we feel that a design is ugly, dissonant and out of place, probably many will agree with us. Good architecture is not an acquired taste. It should still be easily recognisable in terms of proportions, scale and sympathy of materials. Unfortunately, we are not given the opportunity to recognise it so often nowadays. Having said all that, however - and it needs to be said - this is a field, indeed a mine-field, into which we will venture only with extreme caution.

Even after 1960, there were to be wholesale clearances, in which much that would now be considered well worth saving perished along with the not so good. But there were by that time those who were showing increasing concern at the disappearance of many of our historic buildings and ancient street patterns.

The initiative for the foundation of the Nottingham Civic Society came from Arnold J. Pacey, who was at that time (1961) an architectural student at the University of Nottingham and Chairman of the recently founded Architecture Society at the University. He contacted the Civic Trust and in a letter to them dated 15th July, 1961 he said

> I imagine that such a Society would act as a pressure group concerning all aspects of the visual quality of the city. I feel that there is an urgent need for this kind of activity in Nottingham. The City authorities seem to have no coherent idea of how development should take place. Old buildings are disappearing in a piecemeal

fashion without reference to any criteria of what is valuable and what is not. New buildings are appearing in a chaotic variety of shapes and styles.

The Civic Trust encouraged him and gave him a list of people who, to their knowledge, had shown a similar interest in the formation of a society. Amongst those whom Mr Pacey contacted was Mr F.T. Hartlett, the Editor of the local morning daily newspaper, the Nottingham Guardian-Journal. He replied very sympathetically, though he did express some doubts about the usefulness of such a society. 'However', he said, 'for what my blessing is worth, you have it, and at least you can be assured of having a good press.' He went on to say,

> In my time in Nottingham, which now extends to forty years, the dominance of the builder mentality in the City Council has overwhelmed any timid assertion of historical sense. Always the emphasis has been on replacing the old by the new without any regard for architectural merit or historical association. From the criminal destruction of the Dorothy Vernon house in 1927 to the iniquitous bulldozing of the Collin's Almshouses thirty years later, the aldermen and councillors, as well as their technical and executive officers, have scorned adverse criticism based upon civilised values.

Strong stuff!

Mr E.J. Laws, Art Director and Curator of the Castle Museum and Art Gallery, said

> I sympathise strongly with your views. A Civic Society of the kind you envisage would be an admirable thing. The destruction of old houses of architectural merit is almost a Nottingham Specialty. A city that could destroy Abel Collin's Hospital is capable of anything.

Amongst those who gave their active support was Maurice Barley, at that time Senior Tutor in the Department of Extramural Studies at the University and now Emeritus Professor of Archaeology. He was a founder-member and the first Chairman and has given invaluable help and service throughout the Society's history. He is now our President.

To be fair, there were some less enthusiastic reactions. For instance Professor R.C. Coates, Head of the Department of Civil Engineering at the University, who said 'There has always seemed a grave danger that such bodies may become purely negative and will discourage rather than encourage, good architecture, even though the original intentions were of the best'.

With a strong balance of support, however, Mr Pacey went ahead and the Society was launched in January, 1962. It is interesting that the Vice-Chairman was Mr Brendan Henry, the Managing Director of Jessop and Son, Ltd, the large and prestigious departmental store in the City Centre. Sadly, this direct involvement of industry and commerce did not continue, though the Society has received some financial assistance from local firms, both generally and for special purposes over the years.

Our early history was, I suppose, very similar to that of many another such Society. There was much for us to criticise and we did so, forthrightly, but, I hope, positively and constructively. Many times we were in conflict with the local authority, but we quite quickly came to be recognised as a voice to be listened to. We can thank the expertise of our early Committee members for this. As early as 1962 (in our first year), for instance, we published a survey and report on the Lace Market, a most important and historic area of the old City. This was to be followed some years later by a much more comprehensive examination of the area by a Working Party in which we played a very important part, together with other interested bodies. This Working Party, under the aegis of the City Planning Department and chaired by the Deputy City Planning Officer, published its final Report in 1973 as A Conservation Policy for the Lace Market, as the culmination of several years' work. Around the same time, the Society put out two Reports on 'Planning for People', the first of which Saint Ann's dealt with the problems of a run-down inner-city area and the second Trees examined the place of trees in the urban scene, with particular regard to the sorts of trees to be planted and their siting in different situations.

In April, 1970 a Public Inquiry was held into the City's proposals for an Eastern Bypass and the so-called Sheriff's Way. These were radical plans, part of a forty-year scheme for a ring road affecting the whole of the City. The environmental impact of the proposals would have been enormous. I believe the Society really 'came of age' in that

Inquiry. We were represented by Mr A.E. Telling, of Counsel and our case against the proposals was put by Bob Cullen, a local architect and a prominent member of our Committee, in evidence which was carefully researched and well-argued. Maurice Barley also gave evidence, but on behalf of the Council for British Archaeology. The Nottingham Chamber of Commerce also presented evidence, arguing in favour of the Eastern Bypass but against Sheriff's Way. The Society stood alone in comprehensively urging the rejection of the whole of the proposals. In his Report the following year, the Inspector recommended the rejection of the scheme in its entirety and this finding was accepted by the Minister. The Inspector criticised the City Council for their piecemeal approach to their highway plans. This, he said, might enable the Council at a later date to argue that objections in principle to the plans as a whole had been sufficiently ventilated and thus deprive other property owners who would be similarly affected by the remainder of the highway plan of their opportunity to object. He dwelt on the 'disastrous effect (of the proposals) on the historic central core of the town centre' and also said that 'the effect of the submissions will be to spread a planning blight of greater or lesser degree over a great many properties for an apparently lengthy period ... I am of the opinion that the Nottingham primary highway plan falls short of the best that could be achieved in relation to the City's land use and transportation problems'. He advised a fuller investigation and a 'more comprehensive, bolder and more imaginative approach'. This was a great victory for our case. It was undoubtedly a very important landmark for Nottingham and saved it from the traffic strangulation which befell many other cities at that time, including our neighbours Birmingham and Derby, for instance. In our subsequent comment on the result of the Inquiry, we underlined that 'The Council must make it clear to the general public and particularly to those affected by the Primary Highways Plan, that the Plan is scrapped. Otherwise the uncertainty will persist and uncertainty means planning blight.' We offered to become involved with the City Council in the rethinking of its objectives. With or without us, rethinking undoubtedly took place. The Plan was never resurrected!

Of course, we did not win them all! In December, 1969, for instance, we appeared at a Public Inquiry to oppose the proposal to stop-up Drury Hill, an historic mediaeval street in the heart of the old City, in connection with plans for a large new shopping centre, the Broadmarsh Centre. Our opposition was in vain. That kind of Inquiry is always difficult, of course, because the application is merely for permission to do something which is necessary for the implementation of plans which have already been accepted, in outline if not in detail. Perhaps if we had been stronger at an earlier stage things might have been different. Drury Hill was certainly a grave loss for the City's historic heritage.

Sometimes we are faced with difficult decisions. Conservation simply for conservation's sake is not always the best course in the long run. If we try to preserve everything then obviously nothing will change and we shall find ourselves marooned in an architectural and environmental backwater. So, in 1976, we were very much in two minds about the proposals for the modernisation of the Theatre Royal. It was generally acknowledged that improvements were urgently required. The stage area and artists' dressing rooms were seriously sub-standard and prestigious productions were staying away from Nottingham because of this. The Empire Theatre had already been demolished, clearing land on one side of the Theatre site. But on the other side, the proposals required the demolition of the County Hotel, a prominent and attractive feature of Theatre Square, albeit somewhat run down. The work went ahead and has since been complemented by a new Concert Hall at the rear of the same site, in very modern style. I feel now that the concept has been fully vindicated. It is never easy to marry in new extensions with a prominent and well-known building. This was particularly so in the case of the Theatre Royal with its attractive Victorian Palladian facade. Here the result was achieved by the avoidance of hard 'modern' lines. The extensions are rounded and, I think, discreet. The loss of the County Hotel has given us a splendidly up-to-date live theatre, including greatly improved 'front of the house' facilities. The treatment of the whole project has been a great success. In fact the only dislike I have is for the 'light sculpture' on the Concert Hall, which spoils the modern lines of the building and, in daylight at any rate, looks like a heap of metal scaffold poles abandoned by the builders in a hurried departure from the site!

In 1974, we published a report on the Nottingham and Beeston canal, 'Its Present Condition and its Potentialities as a Public Amenity'. In this, we not only surveyed the environment of the canal and recommended improvements, detailed and directed to particular areas, but we also argued strongly for the towpaths to be freely accessible to the public as of right. We pointed out that, at that time, the only parts of the towpath where the public had a right of way were those where there were public footpaths which either existed at the time the canal was constructed or which had since been created. There were no general rights for leisure walking, picnicking or related activities. We sought to change this situation. The City Council gave us support and after some considerable period of opposition by British Waterways, they conceded the point. So now, as a result of our efforts, not only are the towpaths freely open to the public, but the City Council has carried out very substantial environmental improvements on a number of the sections indicated in our Report.

Our most recent campaign of this nature has been directed towards Wollaton Park. In 1986 we published, in conjunction with the Wollaton Village and Park Conservation Society, a comprehensive report on the present condition of the Park and its buildings. We made many recommendations, short and long term, for improvements both physical and organisational. This Report, entitled 'Fraying at the Edges', has attracted wide interest and publicity and despite scepticism and even opposition expressed by a few Council members, it has encouraged the City Council to set up a working party of senior officers to go into the subject and report back to them.

It was in 1975 that we embarked on a project which was to have a profound influence on our long-term future prestige and activities. For it was then that Andrew Hamilton first proposed that we should undertake to sponsor a programme of excavations at Nottingham Castle. To those who visit Nottingham for the first time and who may know little of its history, Nottingham Castle must be something of a disappointment. Brought up on the legends of Robin Hood, they must be surprised to find, not a mediaeval castle, but the much altered remains of a late 17th century mansion, now housing the municipal museum. The once proud Royal Castle, built on the orders of William the Conqueror, finally came to grief after the Civil War, when it was 'slighted' - i.e., partly demolished - by order of Oliver Cromwell. What then remained was almost totally obliterated by the Duke of Newcastle to build his palatial mansion. Much of the rubble from the castle walls and buildings was thrown into the castle yard and covered with earth to form the present Castle Green. After varying fortunes, the ducal mansion was sacked by a mob in 1831. It remained a gutted shell until 1878, when it was considerably altered and converted by the City Corporation into the first provincial museum of fine arts. We commissioned the Trent and Peak Archaeological Trust to carry out the excavations and set about raising money to finance the project. Voluntary contributions were received, but the key to the enterprise was the opening of our Castle Gatehouse Shop in 1976. The premises were leased to us by the City Council at a peppercorn rent, the only condition imposed being that they must give prior approval to any disbursement of the proceeds from the shop. This condition has never been irksome. The City Council has always given its approval to our proposals, extending latterly to a variety of projects, some of which are mentioned later. The Shop has prospered, under the guidance of Thoresby Bradley and Margaret Harrison, with a devoted band of voluntary helpers. This is a most remarkable achievement. It is one thing to organise a relatively short-term operation, but it is quite another to keep enthusiasm and effort going for over ten years to date. Since 1976 we have spent some £56,000 on the actual excavations, most of it from the proceeds of trading, and there is a further expenditure of some £12,000 for the preparation of the final report for publication. In addition to this the City Council put in approximately £12,000 in the early stages and the Department of the Environment contributed nearly £8,000 for specific work. Much valuable information was obtained from the operations. It is true that we have done no more than 'scratch the surface'. There is so much more buried under Castle Green, but this does not detract from the worth of the work that was done and would not have been attempted but for our initiative. It is not every amenity society that has the opportunity for enterprises such as this, of course, but our example may inspire others to look at their local potentialities again.

It was in 1969 that the City Council designated nine Conservation Areas, following the procedure laid down in the Civic Amenities Act 1967. There have been further designations since that time and although we are still arguing for certain additional areas to be designated, virtually the whole of the environmentally sensitive areas of the City are now covered. Subsequently, the Council set up a Conservation Areas Advisory Committee, with representation from a number of amenity societies in the

City, including ourselves. I know the value of such Committees has been questioned by societies in some parts of the country, but I feel that our local Committee makes a positive and helpful contribution to the planning process. The powers of such Committees are purely advisory: they can only recommend, but they provide an informed forum for the initial consideration of planning applications and if they achieve unanimity, as they quite often do, then their voice is respected by the Planning Authority in our experience.

Amenity Societies owe their existence, more often than not, to some burning issue of public controversy at the time of their formation. Our certainly did. We have encountered - and countered - several such issues since then. But an amenity society cannot exist on causes celebres alone. Much of its 'watchdog' activity will be devoted to the day-to-day, almost routine, scrutiny of planning applications and environmental proposals. It must find a place and a positive role in the environmental framework. This means that it should - indeed must - establish a positive, even friendly, relationship with the Planning Department. This does not inhibit vigorous opposition when this is required, but a continuously abrasive relationship is, in my view, quite unnecessary and counter-productive.

Of course, Councils and their Committees can be wayward at times. They may even come to decisions contrary to their Officers' recommendations, sometimes with strange consequences. We have recently been involved in such a case, which is worth recounting as an example of how not to operate the planning process! There is, in the centre of Nottingham, in a Conservation Area, a most unusual Victorian factory building, now disused, called Lambert's Factory. This was threatened with demolition in 1979 and indeed a successful prosecution was mounted by the City Council following partial, unauthorised demolition. In response to representations from ourselves and other concerned bodies, the building was listed (with the support of the City Council, of course). More recently, the County Council prepared plans to use an adjacent site for new magistrates' courts for the City Bench. Then, with that scheme at an advanced stage, with a starting date agreed by the Home Office, they changed their minds in favour of a much more ambitious scheme to include new courts for the County Bench also. In their view, though this is arguable, the new scheme required a larger site. The proper course would have been to seek an alternative and more ample site. It was well-known that at least one such site existed and could readily have been acquired. Instead, they chose to purchase the site including Lambert's Factory, with the express intention of seeking to demolish it! It is worth noting that although the building was disused, a perfectly valid proposal had been put forward for its conversion to an hotel. A Public Inquiry was held into the proposed demolition of a listed building. We contested the proposal most vigorously, taking the initiative, but with the help of other interested bodies. Our case was very ably presented by Andrew Hamilton, our immediate past-chairman, who is a barrister-at-law. The City Council sat on the fence, their hands tied by political relationships, and contrary to the apparent views of their Officers. The Inspector, in his Report, completely accepted our representations and recommended the rejection of the County Council's application. This was confirmed by the Minister for the Environment. The result is a great encouragement for us and for other Amenity Societies. It demonstrates that even a large and powerful local authority can be restrained from flouting all the rules of good planning and environmental control. Fortunately, that sort of thing does not often happen!

With the tapering off of expenditure on the excavations programme, it became possible to think of other projects to which we could turn our hand. These have included major contributions for floodlighting the ancient parish church of St. Mary in the Lace Market (£500) and the restoration of Green's Mill (£4,000). Very recently we have given £5,000 to encourage the provision of a high standard of street furniture in the refurbishment of the Old Market Square. We also actually donated litter bins for the improvement scheme on Castle Road (ca. £600).

A further most interesting development, with great potential for the future, was our very recent restoration of the 18th century boathouse in Wollaton Park. We paid for materials (assisted by a grant from the City Council) and the labour was provided by the Manpower Services Commission under an agreement with the Family First Projects Agency. The success of this project and the good relations we have established with that Agency have encouraged us to consider further projects to be carried out in the same way. With our present Chairman, John Severn, as Consulting Architect, we have set up a Special Projects

Group to look after these schemes. We have been engaged in restoring three historic icehouses in Wollaton Park and one at Clifton and also restoring the ancient dovecote in Wollaton village - reputed to be the oldest in the county, dating from the sixteenth century. There are other ideas in the pipeline and this is obviously going to be an important part of the Society's future activities.

I have said nothing so far about those activities which we share in common with most amenity societies. We now have nearly 900 members. For them we organise a programme of evening meetings with a wide range of notable speakers on subjects related to conservation, the environment, architecture, planning and design. In the summer we arrange visits to places of environmental or historic interest. These visits are aimed at our general membership and so they are selected for a measure of popular appeal.

During the summer months we also run a regular programme of tours and walks for the general public, notably tours of the Castle and Heritage Walks taking in the Shire Hall, the Lace Market and Georgian Nottingham, Swine Green and Sneinton, St. Mary's and the Saxon Settlement, and the Park and Canal Trail. These are in the charge of Cliff Deane, who is also our indefatigable membership secretary. There are other organisations in the City who also organise walks and tours, particularly tours of the various interesting cave systems around the City centre.

All these events, meetings and visits, are generally well supported. I suppose our only possible regret is the comparatively small number of younger people we have attracted into membership. We are by no means alone in this, but it must give rise to some concern for the future of societies such as ours.

Most societies publish a newsletter several times a year. This can be a simple duplicated sheet in the case of the smaller societies, or it can be something more elaborate. Much depends on the resources of the individual society. It also depends on having someone with the special skills and inclination for the job. It can be a very demanding task. We have been very fortunate in finding such a person. Ken Brand, who has now performed this function for several years, has brought to it a professionalism that has brought great credit to the Society. He also looks after our publications, notably the series of eight 'Get to Know Nottingham' booklets, of which he actually wrote three.

Talking of publications, I should also mention the production of 'Nottingham Now', by Maurice Barley and Robert Cullen, published in 1975. This was produced to coincide with European Architectural Heritage Year. It is a profusely illustrated, detailed and authoritative assessment of Nottingham's architectural heritage, quite outstanding in quality and a book of which any amenity society could be proud. We dedicated it 'to the Boots Company Limited in recognition of its contribution to the growth of Nottingham and in gratitude for substantial assistance towards the publication'.

Our links with the Civic Trust have continued and have been strengthened in the past three years by their setting up of an annual, nation-wide Environment Week. This is now well established. Societies are urged to make special efforts during that week to publicise themselves. The Civic Trust gives its support and encouragement with publicity material and space in its magazine, 'Heritage Outlook'. We have responded with special walks for the general public, an architectural quiz and in 1986 a prestigious event at Wollaton Park to mark the completion of the restoration of the boathouse and the restoration of the dovecote, also at Wollaton Park, by the Nottinghamshire Building Preservation Trust, with which we had been associated. Lord and Lady Middleton, whose family built Wollaton Hall in the sixteenth century and who lived there until the 1920s, when the Hall and Park were purchased by the City Council, were our guests of honour.

In 1987, we held a special exhibition in the Old Market Square in Nottingham, featuring local environmental issues and housed in a purpose-built exhibition kiosk.

Country-wide, many hundreds of events are organised by amenity societies to mark Environment Week, involving many thousands of people.

To mark its 30th Anniversary, the Civic Trust convened a highly successful Conference in London in October, 1987, associated with a large and well-staged exhibition of over 100 stands, featuring commercial firms and other bodies in the conservation field. A number of new initiatives was put forward aimed at enhancing the scope and value of the work of the Trust. Certainly, after thirty years, the Trust is very much alive and ready to move with the times.

So, although I have used the Nottingham Civic Society as an illustration of the work being done, I think it is clear that amenity societies throughout the land are in good heart and, in their various ways, doing a very good job for the general improvement of the environment in the widest sense. As a nation, we have always been able to depend greatly on voluntary workers and our community has been wonderfully enriched thereby. Long may this continue.

Chapter Seven

THE INSITE TRUST. PLACES, PERSONS AND THE PROFESSIONAL: LEARNING AND TEACHING FOR HERITAGE

Marista M. Leishman

'History is very many stories'. A well-known Scottish historian made this remark about Falkland Palace in Fife, royal hunting lodge of the Stewart kings. If he had been Teilhard de Chardin (as quoted in the editorial of the June 1980 issue of Teaching History) he would have called it 'the hominization of history'. These two views travel easily together: history is stories about people: people motivated then much as they are today, duly confounding the supposition that events move forward on mechanistic principles; that the operations of cause and effect are carried out in a logical manner; that the pattern is order, control, and predictability; that rational man behaves in a rational manner; for diversion, intervention and irregularity are the norm and at the very heart of what is, there is its opposite; destructiveness at the heart of creativity, self-interest and advancement within altruism, acquisitiveness within generosity and bigotry within wisdom and percipience. Mankind is the endless variable, set in the midst of certain constants. Human consistency does exist however; and man has always been engaged in moulding his environment, in building, and in the manufacture of objects useful or beautiful for himself. He has built for protection and defence, for warmth and shelter or for the exercise of religion. And he has made tools for existence: for cultivation of the soil, for resting, for eating and for clothing. We value these material signs of earlier times: the Standing Stones of Callanish in the Hebrides remain, like Stonehenge, surrounded by the ghosts of their past and the perplexities of their researchers; the crown of St Giles Cathedral still rides high above Edinburgh's Old Town as when with skill and artistry it was devised 500 years ago; and at Crathes Castle in Kincardineshire is the treasured hunting horn of Robert the Bruce.

All these indicators of history: how do we in imagination get in touch with that elusive past of which they are the tangible survivors? To ask how we can connect with the past is also to be considering why we should - because many people would say that history is only marginally important or at its best of academic interest.

First, therefore, we shall look at the capability of artefacts and documents to provide a narrative of the past. Our approach will be by way of the personal and intuitive as opposed to the scientific. We shall consider some philosophical problems arising from the way in which we perceive objects - and also the exclusive approach that we have adopted to seeing things, at the expense of other sense data.

Objects make a decisive contribution to our early life experience - we shall look at that, too, and the way in which this makes for adults a vivid reconnection with the historical perspective when it is presented in museums and historic houses and in the industrial landscape. There is controversy, however, around the question of just what should be preserved from the past and whether the relics of all strata of society are suitable applicants. There is a 'sense of place', however, which is more closely associated with the living and working scenes of the industrial landscape.

From the place quickly follow associations with the people; and it is the people who staff the properties and places that we come to see who play so significant a part in access and enjoyment to them by the public. This being so, training must be seen as a necessary part of any guide's equipment for the job - which is the task undertaken by the Insite Trust. Training, how and by whom, is described.

The positive narrative capability, therefore, of relics extends beyond the presentation of a precise collection of scientific data. This was particularly exciting to Ruskin who found in them not only the stamp of their own beguiling power to survive but the slow yield of the signs of the individuality of their creators through artistry and craftsmanship and infinite attention to detail. Ruskin wrote about them in The Stones of Venice (1935:35): in these artefacts he detected the hand, and the story of the craftsmen who fashioned them. He extracted from them evidence of the 'love and the thoughts of the workman' as

being of greater importance than the actual loveliness of
the thing produced:

> For we have a worthier way of looking at human than
> divine architecture: much of the value both of
> construction and decoration, in the edifices of men,
> depends upon our being led by the thing produced or
> adorned, to some contemplation of the thing created. I
> wish the reader to note this especially; we take
> pleasure or should take pleasure, in architectural
> construction altogether as the manifestation of an
> admirable human intelligence; it is not the strength, nor
> the size, nor the finish of the work which we are to
> venerate: rocks are always stronger, mountains always
> larger, all natural objects more finished: but it is the
> intelligence and resolution of man in overcoming
> physical difficulty which are to be the source of our
> pleasure and subject of our praise. And again, in
> decoration or beauty, it is less the actual loveliness of
> the thing produced, than the choice and invention
> concerned in the production; which are to delight us;
> the love and the thoughts of the workman more than his
> work; his work must always be imperfect, but his
> thoughts and affections may be true and deep.

The attitude which treats the occupants of the
landscape of heritage as interesting material isolates,
engaged in a form of materialistic solipsism, is insufficient.
For their true worth exists in their capacity to act as
pointers and guidelines to the society from which they
sprang, suggestions of the people who fashioned them and of
the lives they lived. The Horn of Leys at Crathes is
remarkable in its survival, beautiful in its craftsmanship;
but prodigious in its historical accumulation.

The task of any of the many heritage bodies of today in
caring for so much historical evidence on behalf of the
nation is to look to the stage beyond, to the observation of
whole areas of living of which they are representative, in
which they are active as indicators and from which can,
with care, be discerned descriptive signs of the past. These
signs provide points of stability in our imaginative re-
creation of that past. The artist and the poet, therefore, can
connect the things of the past with the actual people who
produced them: can help us to see them not as a dead
procedure or part of today's assembly line approach but as

carrying the idiosyncracies of individual creativity.

But is it possible to release such a thing as a positive narrative capacity? It is true that a good deal has been achieved over the years by simply offering the opportunity to look at things, while at the same time providing for their protection against wear or theft. This has meant, however, that seeing and seeing only - has become all important, and has been assumed on its own to be able to provide sufficient evidence without any other form of contact.

There is a cultural precedent at work here of which the opening of historic houses to the public and the workings of museums and their collections is only one example. In those great houses, for instance, the emphasis on seeing has become so great that some rooms that were never meant to be looked at but only to be used are now presented in an uneasy combination of the two: kitchens, sculleries and pantries which were minor industries within the domestic complex of the great house, now demonstrate utensils polished out of all recollection of use, and arranged, sometimes foolishly, as ornaments: egg beaters, spirtles, bannockturners and griddles are lined up with the military precision of the 'Kitchen Goes to War'; the copper batterie de cuisine is placed with stunning exactitude in order of size on the purpose-built shelf, each gleaming pan with attendant lid; and, unsullied by mud and earth the perfectly-formed wax vegetables gleam from rustic baskets. No self-respecting grub or maggot assailed the glowing pears close by. Above the electric flame six vitrified oatcakes endlessly bake and the carcases of rabbit, hare and pheasant hang in dismal proximity to the heat.

It is this cultural programme of seeing at the expense of touching and feeling and smelling that we have fallen heir to. Such an emphasis is no new thing, for it is to be found rooted deeply in everyday language.

'Oh, I see', we say when comprehension breaks. When we promise to 'take a look at' that situation, we are not necessarily expecting to scrutinize a topographical arrangement. An opinion is presented as being 'in that person's view': and indeed, if you close your eyes for a moment and think where you are you will find that picture behind your eyes. What we cannot see we imagine and even that word comes from an image or picture. As we 'envisage' an event taking place, we 'focus' our attention on it. So we form a picture of its occurrence in our mind. Seeing is apparently all.

And then along come the inventors and they turn their attention to improving scientific precision through sight. This is particularly true of the medical world where enlightened minds find ways of seeing things that are otherwise invisible, and the instruments that help them to do that they generally call a '...scope'. In the nineteenth century the auroscope reflected candlelight into a mirror with a central hole, through which the operator peered to see into the ear; it had been preceded by the eye machine or opthalmoscope. Many other 'scopes' appeared; but the stethoscope, which doesn't actually look, but listens, does so in order to help the practitioner build up a medical picture in his mind's eye.

All these clever people and their inventions in the cause of medicine were preceded in time and prioritized in status by Copernicus, who, instead of focusing down, sought to extend his vision to the galactic bounds - and met trouble as a result.

These men believed in vision as the most important of the senses. Is that so?

But for the blind person there must be some other way. He must find out that other code of rich signals waiting to be interpreted: weight, texture, form, temperature, smell, resistance or pliability, adaptation to another surface, parts in relation to parts or the capacity to generate activity and sounds. In the same great house kitchen there may be a mincing machine fixed to the table. Allowed to investigate we find that some parts are static to allow others to be mobile and operational. The machine works by cause and effect: rotate the handle and parts move for an obvious purpose. The metal is cold and resistant; the handle different and less so. The shapes are purposeful. By touching and working it we understand more about it.

But the testimony of language, the generations and those who must depend on other senses is not enough for the philosopher, who takes an unusual, some might say jaundiced, look at things about him. Of his own table Bertrand Russell (1951:8) says:

> To the eye it is oblong, brown and shiny ... and although I believe the table is 'really' of the same colour all over, the parts that reflect the light look much brighter than the other parts, and some parts look white because of reflected light. I know that if I move, the parts that reflect the light will be different, so that the apparent

distribution of colours on the table will change ...

Here we have already the beginning of one of the distinctions that cause most trouble in philosophy - the distinction between 'appearance' and 'reality', between what things seem to be and what they are. Thus - our supposedly inoffensive table is giving rise to some uncertainty and we now doubt the testimony of the sense of sight. We can no longer say with certainty that this is its colour - after all the colour will be different by artificial light, or to a colour-blind person, and in the dark there will be no colour at all. The colour changes according to these, and plenty more circumstances, and colour is no longer an inherent characteristic of the table. Seeing, in fact, is not, perhaps believing, after all.

From looking at things, therefore, our information is going to be incomplete. At the very least we are going to be misinformed. But the sight of a thing is not the only source of information available to us; and in order to gather more and confirmatory information we should be able to handle and get its feel as well, even if only to clarify or amplify the partial and conflicting evidence of the eyes. So let's try the sensation of touch. Coming back to the philosopher's table we will not be surprised to meet with more difficulties.

> With the naked eye one can see the grain, but otherwise the table looks smooth and even. If we looked at it through a microscope, we should see roughnesses and hills and valleys, and all sorts of differences imperceptible to the naked eye. Which of these is the real table?
>
> (Russell 1951:10)

Thus, if there is a real table - and of course the philosopher will wonder if there really is one there at all - it is not the same as what we immediately experience by sight or touch or hearing (because if knocked, it will give off different sounds in different circumstances.) What is to be known?

It's worth a tentative excursion into the philosopher's field if only to remind ourselves that informationally we're in a muddle. Being, at our best, naturally inquisitive and looking for more and better ways of knowing, we will certainly want to adjust the evidence of one set of sense-data - in this case the things that we learn through looking -

135

to those of another and see if by checking one against another our information is less incomplete and more interesting.

In a museum, therefore, it's frustrating only to be able to see and even then often through a glass case. Recently the British Museum laid on an exhibition called 'The Human Touch', Victoria Neumark reviewing it in the Times Educational Supplement wrote: 'what an amazing force one primitive sense, touch, has for us human beings ... the pieces seem to come alive at the touch'. Whether the Curator had read his Russell or not I don't know: but even if he hadn't, he knew that one set of senses is incomplete in the information that it gives and that others have to be called upon to supplement the experience and to kindle the imagination.

An important book has been written by Marion Milner (1950:10) called On Not Being Able to Paint. In the book Milner describes how since early childhood she had always longed to paint but had found that the skill eluded her. In teaching and in books the requirement seemed to be to represent adequately the forms and shapes and colours before her, and to attend particularly to outline. Baffled in her attempts she began to realise that the imaginative mind could have strong views of its own on the meanings of light, distance, darkness and so on, and that the apparently all-important question of outline had to be considered in relation to other modes of presentation. This was particularly true of perspective drawing.

It occurred to her that 'it all depended upon what aspects of objects one was most concerned with':

> It was as if one's mind could want to express the feelings that come from the sense of touch and muscular movement rather than from the sense of sight. In fact it was almost as if one might not want to be concerned, in drawing, with those facts of detachment and separation that are introduced when an observing eye is perched upon a sketching stool ... it seemed one might want some kind of relation to objects in which one was much more mixed up than that.

Then she goes on to deal with outline, and the emphasis traditionally given to it. For she:

> had always assumed in some vague way that outlines were 'real'. In a book about drawing, however she read

that 'from a visual point of view ... the boundaries (of masses) are not always clearly defined, but are continually merging into the surrounding mass and losing themselves, to be caught up again later on and defined once more. (ibid 15)

Milner says that outlines put objects in their places:

We seem to believe that they (the outlines) are real despite the fact that they are 'the one fundamentally unrealistic, non-imitative thing in this whole job of painting'. (ibid p. 17) But because the outline represents the world of fact, of separate, touchable, solid objects, to cling to it is surely to protect oneself against the other world: the world of imagination'. We need, that is to say, to be 'much more mixed up in the objects' than simply, and in a detached way, to look at them and trace their outlines. The human and the personal and imaginative need to get together with them.

And so the artist, as well as the philosopher, is saying that the world around us is only truly known by the exercise and the evidence of all the senses.

People coming to many museums and houses open to the public have to acquire as much experience as they can from seeing only in the hope that their historical imagination can make something of this limited data. Much as in the way that it was available to Thomas Hardy in his poem 'Old Furniture'.

I see the hands of the generations
That owned each shiny familiar thing
In play on its knobs and indentations,
And with its ancient fashioning
Still dallying:

Hands behind hands, growing paler and paler
As in a mirror a candleflame
Shows images of itself, each frailer
As it recedes, though the eye may frame
Its shape the same.

We would probably all agree that objects do signify for us; but why? We are surrounded by them: the utilitarian and dull, like this half-worn pencil, the beautiful and decorative

- a flower study is on the wall, and the object which is both beautiful and useful: see this fine contemporary wooden sideboard. Objects figure - and draw much of their significance for us as a result - from our early childhood experience of them. Indeed it has been shown how many of our aptitudes and capacities are laid down in childhood, in the very early days before ever-conscious memory played its part. Young babies become fascinated by a particular toy, perhaps a woolly bear. The bear is clearly special and signifies more than other toys. It could be, that in claiming so much affectionate energy, some special line of discovery, especially self discovery, is going on. The psychoanalyst D.W. Winnicott says (1971:13) that 'from birth the human being is concerned with the problem of the relation between what is objectively perceived and what is subjectively conceived of': there is, in other words, an outer reality: the world outside - objects, sounds, sights - and an inner reality: the continuing person in the midst of these things. In his chapter 'Transitional Objects and Transitional Phenomena' Winnicott argues that there is 'me' and there is 'not me'. These are two realities and they must be brought into relation with each other. Something is needed to demonstrate to the 'me' that there is a world which is 'not me' out there; to represent, as it were, the whole great world of otherness and to modify the world of endless subjectivity. The woolly bear comes to represent the external world as being apart from and negotiable by 'me'. And - in clarifying the objective world outside, so is confirmation made of the subjective world of which 'I' am the centre. This is the essential central self-affirmation, necessary to us all.

Play with this object, which Winnicott calls the 'transitional object' becomes the stimulus for creative play. It is the starter for cultural life. The successful transition from the subject-dominated empire to subject in relation to object and external reality is the source of creative living; it is the source of the feeling that life is worth living. The experience of a personal psychic reality which is the basis of the sense of self, comes through objects, through the control of objects and through, as a result, the feeling of magic in discovering the separated individual in his own self-hood.

If people are going to think historically they have to be able to be in touch with these early experiences where the object signifies, the subject is confirmed, and creativity explodes into life. As sentient intellectual people we need the proximity and direct experience of environmental memorials to allow access to the scope of the historic present.

The most telling expression of an era is often when its artefacts are still in place. From this they acquire context and the kind of definition which is possible only when they are seen in relation to other exhibits and allowed to cohere in a related working location. This is a bonus which becomes more accessible to us as urban and industrial life is beginning to be recognized as worthy of preservation and study. But this change is not coming about without controversy: opposition is well orchestrated.

'Romancing the grime', the Guardian called the latest bid to turn 100 acres of soot and gasworks around Kings Cross station into a giant theme park. Its purpose would be to illustrate London's industrial past, memorializing the battered sheds from which the city was supplied with coal, potatoes, bricks and fish. In a book called The Heritage Industry Robert Hewison (1987:29-32) expresses his dismay at the way in which we are re-building the past in a cosy fantasy of itself; and Waldemar Januszczak in the Guardian roundly poses the question: 'What kind of sophisticated museum double-talk enables a society to present an era of such abject misery, squalor, dirt, disease, exploitation, child cruelty in so rosy a light that 'it' can be passed off fondly as the real Britain, occasional sadnesses and all?'

Since this represents changed direction in the heritage industry, and since change of any kind is nearly always controversial, it is not to be wondered at that the re-creation of the industrial past has critics. But it comes nevertheless as a welcomed initiative in the face of decades in which the heritage has been presented in terms of what it is able to measure up to in terms of certain imposed standards of quality.

The criteria which are selected, and on the basis of which a building, for instance, is deemed to qualify for public access - or to fail - are those in which, more often than not merit is equated with status. It is the privileged minority who live in great houses and collect beautiful things, and for whom rarity is a value in itself and the accumulation of rich things as to a shrine a natural activity. The emphasis placed on this particular kind of qualification does much, certainly, to illuminate an abundant and diverse cultural resource. It also helps to confirm a sometimes flagging identity around ownership with the unfailing opportunities to indulge in the individualistic, if not the idiosyncratic. But it does leave unattended the need to differentiate between a value that neglects a whole social section and cultural inheritance at the expense of a much smaller and very different one. The section, that is, which is proletariarized and follows up both the industrial and the rural scenes - the latter through museums of farming life and cottage industries re-created.

This means that there are far more of the houses of those who prospered or who inherited available for the public to see than the houses or the artefacts of those who didn't.

Equally many more of the objets d'art collected by the privileged are on show in museums than are the utilities which would have been in the hands of the labouring others. A charge of elitism could, until very recently, have been levelled at the museums also where qualification for exhibition, or for inclusion in the collection, rested on rarity, craftsmanship or antiquity - probably in that order - and where utility and generality scarcely figured.

It is as well that a change is at work here.

The move in favour of a reflection of the lives and conditions of ordinary people is supported by a growing consciousness of the significance of the social sweep: that the portrayal of a selected and priviledged part of it will not do; and that the role of a custodian of heritage is to take in also the industrial landscape whose concomitants are functional, purpose built, production intended, worker orientated. Beauty and significance are not here other than in the form of utility, constancy and familiarity. How much of the human component, to which Ruskin refers, can they have?

All of us have a sense of place, of personal identity with a locus, a place for roots. They call it 'topofilia' and it belongs as much to the scene of the smoke stacks as to the marbled hall. An environmental attachment grows up which has been defined by the geographer Y.F. Tuan (1974) as including '... all of the human being's affective ties with the material environment.' Many of these feelings arise because a place 'is home, the centre of memories and the means of gaining a livelihood'. Topofilia is enriched by history: in other words it is nourished by incident, and by events which are known: 'the appreciation of the landscape is more personal and longer lasting when it is mixed with the memory of human incidents ... this new insight into the real is sometimes experienced as beauty'. Within that scene there will be a building on which emotions may particularly focus, the incarnation of something large and close to lives. Buildings and places have a spirit and a quality which, although unique to every individual, are yet intrinsically bound up with the process of their own maturation - the connection, in short, is with home, with childhood and with parenting. And beauty, elegance, decor and the arts do not necessarily have any part in this. But familiarity does.

The industrial landscape - the smoke stacks, the gas coolers and the steelworkers' houses are as emotionally binding for some as the giant portico, the elegant clock on the stable wing or the brass-studded green-baize door to the servants' wing for others. But while we agree to preserve the latter our civic leaders rush in to erase the former, and, as they would hold, all memory of it. They have a theory, which has never actually been substantiated, that the workers in steel and other industries now died, hated the old industrial environment, and supported all signs of it swept away. This was, however, a useful idea to which to hold when elected and appointed leaders were attracted by the possibilities of stamping their own identity on an area and creating a new shining civic image.

> Some of these elite people had come into the communities from outside, and saw the old and deteriorating mills as symbols of economic stagnation. For them salvation lay not only in renewing the physical fabric but also in changing the image ... the problem is that they are motivated to destroy them precisely because it is the cultural and historical messages inherent in these buildings which they wish to erase.

So writes Randolph Langebach (1984:466) and those things which, in fact, the people want to preserve. And the trouble is too that the people to whom these things matter are largely inarticulate, a population long rooted in the area but not experienced in forming views and speaking. Their attachment to their physical environment, the place and buildings on which their lives and livelihood have depended is unexpressed, perhaps unrealised, until it is savagely swept away in the name of progress. In place of the tall tenement houses and cavernous streets which characterized Glasgow come the faceless structures, high, geometrical and impersonal, their facades already disfigured with graffiti and the litter already swirling about the pavements below, a judgement upon them by those whose lives they failed to improve.

In the centre of a vast housing estate in Drumchapel, to the north-west of Glasgow, the planners dreamt up the need for yet another housing unit to occupy the only remaining unused plot. Up until now it had been left, local people assumed, because an old fountain stood there, the only remaining sign of the original village. One day the bulldozers swept in, and in a moment it was gone. The hubbub rose - even though it was too late - and as they protested the people spoke about the value of the monument that symbolized their past and their roots, and, by implication, their future.

In discussing the industrial landscape and the emotional investment that is assigned to it by its own people we have not severed the thought connection with Ruskin nor strayed as far as might appear from the closeness of the ties between objects and our psychic inheritance, between objects and parenting and the thesis of Winnicott; or between objects, scenes, locations and childhood in the midst.

Nor, after all, have we lost sight of the personal. In the same way as the derivation of the word 'parson' is thought to come from 'person' - that is, the person in the midst of the parish - so the person signifies in the midst of the collection, or the building or the historic site. As interpreters the people are the builders of bridges between the exhibit and the visitor, between the place - the topos - and his experience of it, between the content and the level at which the visitor is enabled to respond to it.

This is particularly true of children and young people, who, if they are going to relate to figures of the past, must themselves be permitted to signify in the present, encountering personally and by introductions those who are going to act as their interpreters and guides. The spontaneous curiosity of children is their point of contact with the people of history: their discovery of objects and artefacts of 300 years ago must not be dimmed with the communication of a repressive reverence for their antiquity. There is a thin dividing line here between respect: the healthy regard for proper worth and significance, a lively interaction between observer and object; and reverence, that unquestioning attitude imposed upon a glazed and submissive group. The unilateral declaration of antiquity stills the capacity for questioning and enjoyment, without which little learning follows. The guides and interpreters at the site are the people who, for the time being, personify that site for the visitor and are the substance of his favourable, or less than favourable impression of it. We tend to remember people and the way in which they treat or receive us more distinctly than the places or objects themselves. A great deal rests on this rather surprising fact, and it makes the role a demanding one.

It is a role filled by people titled variously as room steward, guide, custodian, warden or steward. They have a central task, which is responsibility for security. After that, the degree to which they are expected to relate to the public, and the manner of their so doing, is less than clear, many feeling that to encourage fraternization is to risk theft. Nevertheless it is recognized that the security officer whose sole task is as guard is a threatening presence and a negative one; and some of the larger institutions are attempting to add an extra dimension to the job with encouragement to relate to the visitor. The intention is good, but the carrying out is harder, especially for those who have been schooled for one activity and attitude. Others are expected to offer information, welcome, and surveillance in equal measure - all while stationed in one area; others again are guides to parties and groups on properties where visitors may not wander at will - a requirement which naturally gives rise to resentment. Whatever their title the interpreters - as it is best to call the people on the spot - have a many-faceted job, and what follows as a task description only occasionally admits exaggeration.

Interpreters are the people who combine the role of security officer with that of the instant historian; who are publicists for the property as well as tourist officers for the locality; and who can grasp architectural history and also arrange flowers. Interpreters are traffic wardens and art historians, cloakroom attendants and landscape gardeners. They are people who understand that Upstairs Downstairs does not, after all, provide a summary of the social historians' field, but that to be a platform speaker as well as an expert in textile restoration is amongst the requirements of the adequate interpreter. It is desirable to be an audio-visual technician and a practitioner in the art of drama and role play; and that to understand the burglar-alarm systems as well as the herd instinct in the public (through the application of first principles of psychology) are not only desirable but essential attributes.

As both sheep-dog and prophet, the eyes of all are upon the interpreter: and for this reason it is better not to appear as a model from Top Shop nor as a representative from Jaeger, because the interpreter has an important role as shopkeeper.

But the good interpreter has one more asset, and without it the rest are of no great account. It is the art of communication. No amount of information readily available, no impressive collection of skills or reserves of self-confidence and resourcefulness are of much use unless the interpreter and the visitor are in touch with one another. Visitors are all different and each comes with their own individual apparatus of expectation, enjoyment and experience.

But if the audience is imprisoned in boredom and stunned with the impact of gratuitous and unsolicited information, the merits of those many buildings or collections through which history seeps and which are distinguished in architecture and articulate about an era and a style are of little account. Therefore, a good interpreter is a good listener long before he or she is an effective speaker or sensitive responder to the half-formed question.

Every season 200 million visitors find their way to the attractions which at all levels and of all kinds are waiting to receive them; of the many thousands of guides, stewards and custodians, some receive training and preparation for the task; and of those sites which tackle the task with care and attention, only a few attend to the questions of communication and the fostering of good relations with the public. Too many interpreters are left to get informed and then to rub along; and the elusive questions about the art of relating well and effectively to visitors don't arise.

Now that the task is beginning to the recognized for the significance that it has, it is acknowledged that questions of training, preparation and support for guides need to be properly addressed. In this sensitive area of primary historical source material (as well as this multi-million pound industry) the public needs to be in the hands of people who, as well as having great goodwill, have criteria for performance and standards of communication to which to aspire; and who are used to having their work scrutinized. Only the highest professional standards are appropriate, for, without them both interpreters and the public get dissatisfied. The first are deprived of the achievement which follows hard preparation and accreditation and the second become irritated and feel short changed at being faced with amateurism.

The combination which follows does less than justice to the riches of the heritage and leaves largely unavailable, or greatly reduced, the impact of a noble accumulation of history. Amateurism amongst staff is especially inappropriate with the realization that heritage is not, after all, nostalgia, but the continuum for learning and understanding which stretches in a long line into the future as well as gathering in the significant past, capturing both in an important present. The form of the present is that in which experience arises from the interaction of the historic environment and its interpreter upon the imagination and intellect, together engaged in the constructive activity of interrogating the past.

Every guide, interpreter, receptionist and salesperson, becomes irrevocably identified in the mind of the visitor with the place in which they work. Staff are therefore in a very influential position in regard to visitors and can mould their view of their experience - persuading them to recommend and to return - or to do neither.

Because of this situation the Insite Trust has been formed to train staff who work in all kinds of visitor attractions and to provide them with the communication and social skills that they need. The attendant in the art gallery, for instance, who is responsible for security is very clear about this. But he is less clear about the importance of not letting it show; vigilance and suspicion are a hostile environment for the visitor. The room steward in the historic house should tell the visitor what he wants to know - without adding a great deal more about which he has not enquired. Being bored and trapped are risks visitors still have to take. Some decide the risks are too great.

Cathedral stewards who are there ostensibly to provide a welcoming presence but often are at a loss to know how to go about it: the question about the extent to which they are there actually to proselytize is not fully resolved in their minds. And the girl in the self-service restaurant may feel that her encounter with members of the public is of such little consequence that it doesn't matter how she performs or how she looks, or what are her gestures and attitude. Nobody has told her that attitude counts and that no matter how tiny the transaction the message of welcome or rebuff is conveyed with total accuracy.

Staff development courses by Insite, therefore, are going on in places as various as palaces, castles, historic houses, museums of many kinds, theme parks and in the shops and restaurants associated with them.

There is a rising tide of agreement in favour of the expansion of the task and the recognition of the public dimension to every role: Insite attempts to meet this new demand.

Then follows the much-needed estimate of the nature of the requirement and the readiness or otherwise to meet it by staff whose aptitude varies according to attitude, experience, and conditioning. And for whom training, when it has been available, has been for certain prescribed responsibilities in which social and interpretative responsibilities have not figured.

It is not hard to see therefore that a lot is being asked of the interpreters. And it is equally clear that the cost of expecting them simply to get on with it is too high in terms of the property itself, the burgeoning interest of the public and its accumulated lore from visitor attractions. More people by habit, opportunity and inclination visit more places, become more discerning, more demanding and are in a position, as it were, to begin to look seriously for standards in presentation and to find amateurism in the scene mildly inappropriate.

It is entirely possible, for instance, for a family visit to a historic house to be totally dislocated by the mother being told that she must leave her shoes behind because of the stiletto heels; or a teenager his rucksack. The reasons for the rules may be obvious to staff, but the way in which the visitor is asked to comply needs skill and sensitivity if the encounter is not going to become oppositional. Visitors who feel deeply about these things do not take kindly to being instructed as to what they should look at or what they will find of interest; and those who have only a tentative curiosity will find that it scarcely survives a detailed harangue.

Professional staff development and skills training, therefore, is centred on social skills for the establishing of rapport with visitors and on the expertise that is called for in the selection and management of information so that it comes in at the requisite level. The nature of adult education and the study of the ways in which adults learn, has to be addressed, as well as the kind of information that centres on each resource and its individual management.

Adults seem to learn when they find that the goals and the objectives are realistic and important, that is, that they are related to the job and are obviously useful. Adults like to see results and to have kinds of feed-back that tell them that they are making progress towards a certain goal.

But learning something new, whether it is a skill, or a technique or a concept, may produce anxiety and fear of external judgement, digging up most probably unwelcome impressions of school life. But adults do come to the learning situation with a whole range of experiences, of knowledge, skills, interests and competence. It seems essential therefore, to recognize individuals and what they bring and not to try to educate by hose pipe. Furthermore adults need to be involved in the structuring and nature of their course, of its objectives, contents and activities as well as the forms of its assessment not only apparent to them but in some cases selected. (Perhaps the most effective and far-sighted methods of learning are the self-directed courses presently available from some of the London colleges).

Direct and concrete experience is the best medium through which to learn, especially when what has been learned can be applied. A huge resistance sets in to any learning situation which looks like being an attack on competence. Equally, one that suggests a prescription as to what is needed in this particular case. And when it comes to changing behaviour, always an Everest of a task, abstract talk sessions will not do, but informal situations with social interaction will change the scene. In developing a trainee-centred approach to learning the necessary skills must be identified. They are those centred on the need to listen, to clarify, to give feedback, and to reflect. The management of silence must be learned as well as the establishment of relationships, and precision as to the level of interest and motivation of the visitor and of the management of the response accordingly.

The situation in which the visitor is informationally lost and therefore made to feel inadequate should be avoided: as too, the presence of recriminatory evaluation. There must be sympathetic understanding of ignorance. 'If you do not', said Coleridge 'understand the basis of a man's ignorance, you will remain ignorant of his understanding'.

To these ends the trainers, or consultants who work for Insite must understand the factors which produce effective learning and they must have a selection of strategies on which to draw. They must be able to take account of the experience and motivation of the trainee or trainee group and match learning styles to training methods. Acting as facilitator the trainer must adjust pace, give responsibility by allowing initiative, and make ample provision for feedback to ensure participative learning.

There are various methods, such as monitored work experience, demonstration and practice, group discussion, simulation and role play and case study.

Analysis of the legitimate expectation of the customer for his visit; of the skills needs of staff; of the nature of adult education; and of the goals in training for the consultants has predicated a pattern according to which Insite operates.

First, the training is taken to the site. Staff are not called to go as delegates to a centre but instead to work on familiar territory. This is where ready associations of visitor and staff interaction become a springboard for learning how to do it better.

Second, the training programme is to be worked out in consultation with management with an individual programme resulting; and certainly not as a prescriptive syllabus proposed like a blanket solution.

Third, it is not didactic, but with participants engaged, so to speak, in their own programme for learning.

Learning is achieved through the skill of the consultant using his or her own stranger value in relation to the group: the catalyst in the midst. Emerson knew this when he said: 'It is not instruction but provocation that I receive from another soul'. The field of the heritage as the arena for provocation of this kind is fitting.

And so too a new awareness for interpreters and managers alike of the scope and the significance of the task and of the potential that is not yet fully realized. The significance, that is, of the place, and of the professional person in the midst.

BIBLIOGRAPHY

Hardy, T., (1976:62) 'Old Furniture': Thos. Hardy: An
    Autobiography in Verse, Elaine Wilson and Howard
    Shaw. London: Shepheard-Walwyn
Hewison, R., (1987:27) The Heritage Industry. Britain in a

Climate of Decline, London: Methuen

Januszczak, W., The Guardian, Sept. 1987

Langebach, R., (1984) 'Continuity and Sense of Place' in Mental Health and the Environment, ed. Hugh Freeman, New York: Churchill Livingstone

Milner, M., (1950:10) On Not Being Able to Paint, London: Heinemann Educational (First published 1950 under pseudonym Joanna Field)

Neumark, V., (7.3.86) No. 3636. page 32. Times Education Supplement Scotland, London: Times Newspapers Ltd

Ruskin, J., (1935:35) The Stones of Venice, London: Dent Everyman's Library

Russell, B., (1951) The Problems of Philosophy, pp. 8, 10. London: OUP

Tuan, Y., (1974) Topophilia. A Study of Environmental Perception, Attitudes and Values, Englewood Cliffs: Prentice Hall

Winnicott, D., (1971:13) Playing and Reality, London: Penguin Books Ltd

Conclusion

CULTURE, EDUCATION AND THE STATE

Kenneth Lawson

In this concluding chapter I propose to consider briefly the main senses in which the word 'culture' is used by Matthew Arnold, T.S. Eliot and Raymond Williams. I then argue that when an attempt is made to define and describe a particular culture, we produce an abstraction similar to that produced by an historian who selects and simplifies in order to give an historical account of what in reality was a complex of events. Different perceptions of a culture are possible and different descriptions might emerge from different points of view.

Some of the presuppositions which appear to underlie contemporary British culture are considered and a philosophy of individualism is seen to run through much of our thinking about society, ethics, science and politics. Similar presuppositions are shown to be present in our concept of education.

It is finally argued that our culture is predominantly based upon the idea of 'process' to the neglect of purposes and ideals. This, it is suggested, makes our society more susceptible to political control.

1. THE CONCEPT OF 'CULTURE'

If the term 'culture' is defined in a broad sense, we can all be said to live within a culture of some kind. None the less, the term does not seem to arise naturally in general conversation except at points of crisis or concern. We talk for example of 'culture shock' when someone visits a country which has very different traditions and patterns of behaviour. On occasion we rise to the defence of, say, a threatened building or a work of art on the grounds that they represent or are a part of our 'cultural heritage'. Complaints are made by members of ethnic minorities who believe that the educational system does not give due prominence to minority cultures. Feminists claim that our culture is male orientated. Others claim that education is dominated by middle-class cultural values and they would prefer to give preference to what is called 'working class' culture. Certain kinds of sub-culture such as 'the drug culture', 'pop culture' and 'youth culture' are disparaged by sections of the population who do not subscribe to them.

With such a variety of responses, it might be asked what we mean by the term culture and why it is so important at least to some people and for some of the time. It is the purpose of this chapter, therefore, to explore some aspects of the ways in which we think about the concept of culture, why it seems to be of importance and how it relates to the concept of education.

Most of our general words are ambiguous in that they can convey a range of meanings, the distinctions between which are not always clear. Such words can evoke a range of responses and they are used in a variety of contexts as our examples illustrate. In addition, we each bring our own understandings to bear and words have different connotations depending upon previous experience of their use.

For some people 'culture' signifies such things as the arts, which may be seen either as a bore, or as a priceless heritage depending upon the point of view. The term 'culture' in common with 'education' therefore has an evaluative function which can be used either to disparage or to approve. To describe someone as 'cultured' is on the whole to praise them. To be 'cultured' is to satisfy certain criteria related to interests, commitments and accomplishments and there are expectations of those who satisfy such criteria. Other epithets which could be regarded as close synonyms are 'civilised' and 'educated'. They, along with 'culture' point in a particular direction and it is contradictory to regard someone both as 'cultured' and 'uncivilised'. However, much hinges on the descriptive content of such terms and this is usually the point at which argument and disagreement begin.

Much of the evaluative force of the idea of 'culture' derives from its normative use which Matthew Arnold

151

referred to in <u>Culture and Anarchy</u> (1869 and 1932: 45) as 'a study of perfection'. For him 'It moves by the force, not merely or primarily of the scientific passion for more knowledge, but also of the moral and social passion for doing good'. Arnold then quotes Montesquieu's claim that the purpose of culture is 'To render an intelligent being yet more intelligent'.

Raymond Williams takes a similar stance with what he calls the 'ideal' view of culture as 'a state or process of human perfection in terms of certain absolute or universal values. The analysis of culture, if such a definition is accepted, is essentially the discovery and description in lives and works of those values which can be seen to compose a timeless order, or to have permanent reference to the universal human condition' (Williams, 1961: 57).

Williams's ideal of culture in a timeless sense can include the conventional view of culture as the best in the creative arts but for Arnold culture is more than this. His notion of perfection depends upon two things: reason and the will of God. But perfection needs more than the 'endeavour to see and learn ...' (Arnold, 1932: 46). It needs also the commitment to make it prevail. Culture as perfection therefore becomes a moral imperative and whatever content is associated with the concept, becomes normative.

For Arnold, the descriptive content of culture includes first religion and then art, science, poetry, philosophy and history, by means of which culture becomes 'an internal condition' concerned with the growth of our humanity proper as distinguished from our animality. To those who respond to such clarion calls, 'culture' becomes a term of the highest approbation. For others, the term can be seen as one of abuse, and as Arnold observes, with the English 'the word is always used in a disapproving sense' (Arnold, 1932: 43).

The notion of timeless absolute values is not at all fashionable in an age which seems to give prominence to various forms of relativism, but it should be noted that Arnold's values are actually those which help to define what has come to be called 'Western culture' and they are therefore culturally relative. What seems to make them absolute is the extremely long time span over which they have developed as ideals. They can therefore be brought readily into Williams's rather weaker definition of culture as that which is regarded as best in a specific culture rather than as absolute and timeless. What is at issue between the strong 'ideal' and the weaker 'relative' definition, is the limit within which a specific culture is defined.

Thus far we have been considering the concept of 'culture' as an essentially selective and normative concept. Its use in this sense is therefore commendatory. But in referring to 'culture' as what is best in a 'specific culture', we have actually slipped into a further use of the term which refers to 'culture' as an abstraction from 'a culture' or 'the culture' in a non-evaluative descriptive sense, more in keeping with anthropological and sociological senses of culture as a total way of life. This is the sense in which we can speak of 'Graeco-Roman', 'Polynesian' and 'British' cultures and so on. In a descriptive sense all that is there to be observed may be included. It covers not only 'the best' but also 'the worst'.

The notion of culture as the description of 'a way of life' is not without difficulties, neither is it totally unrelated to normative concepts of culture as both Williams and T.S. Eliot recognised (Eliot, 1948: 22).

A distinction might be made between 'the way in which we live' and the idea of 'a way of life'. The former is purely contingent upon what we actually do from day to day and includes all kinds of trivial actions many of which are unnoticed and unrecorded. In contrast to this 'a way of life' is an abstraction. Like 'culture', 'social class', 'process' and 'event' it is another descriptive category and its meaning derives from the way in which it is defined and the manner in which particular examples are described.

The making of descriptions of any kind is essentially a selective process in which use is made of concepts and general terms deemed appropriate for the purpose. What is appropriate depends on the purpose for which particular descriptions are being made and this determines the mode of description. What is ostensibly the 'same' social event can be described within a political or an economic frame of reference, individual behaviour can be described pyschologically or sociologically and physical objects can be described variously in terms of their chemistry, their physical structure or in aesthetic terms.

The problem of describing 'a way of life' is not dissimilar from the historian's problem. In neither case is there a hard objective phenomenon to be described and in a sense the description actually defines whatever is being described. Historical description is from some point of view, and the terms of the description which are thought to be relevant are a matter of judgement. No description is total, and descriptions can be seen as verbal models or representations. They do not replicate the totality and in this respect they are similar to artists' impressions or scale models of buildings. A model might look like the real thing but close inspection reveals considerable simplification of the details which simply cannot be reproduced on a small scale. Verbal representation is also limited and what are called 'facts' are often highly selected simplifications of observable data chosen for their importance for the task in hand. For the purposes of some kinds of historical description it is important to note how people worked, how they ate and how they dressed. For other purposes it is more important to consider what kings and their ministers said and did or how builders and engineers developed their technologies. Even when these are all put together in a textbook, history is never total.

Similar considerations apply to descriptions of cultures. We start with presuppositions about what constitutes 'ways of life' and we have categories which include the religious, the economic and political, the artistic and so on. Observed behaviour is categorised in some way or other and we look for regularities and patterns rather than freak occurrences and accidents. We tend also to look for salient features which stand out and characterise what seem to be the totality. We talk of 'industrial' and 'post industrial cultures' (or societies), of 'consumer culture' and so on. Each of these is a gross simplification of the ways in which people live and even the concept of 'living' makes qualitative distinctions. It connotes activities such as acquiring and preparing food, securing shelter, and it can be extended to include quite sophisticated conceptions of social organisation and intellectual activity.

The actual descriptive categories applied to describe a culture, are themselves a cultural product and if we are describing our own culture, dominant modes of thought generated within that culture or borrowed from other cultures will reinforce themselves by being built into the presuppositions with which descriptions begin. A culture of a particular kind will therefore produce descriptions of itself which reflect the dominant perceptions of its members. It is almost as if I, being the person that I am, try to describe myself as the person that I am. What I perceive as being significant about myself will enter my description but I have no objective criteria by which to judge what I 'really' am.

My point is simply that any descriptive account of a

culture is a selective account of what is perceived to be important. The values of the describer are reflected in the descriptions given and there is a prescriptive element in what might purport to be a neutral or objective description. The gap between normative and descriptive concepts therefore narrows considerably and we are in the end dealing with a particular type of problem which is inherent in the social sciences generally. We start with concepts or models and these generate importance and significance in what is observed.

. Self-conscious reflection about the way in which we live and attempts to define a total culture are of course comparatively rare. Such activity is more likely to be undertaken by social scientists, journalists and educators than the man in the street. What might be called our 'real culture' is something lived and experienced in a much less formal and unselfconscious way except at points of crisis. We live, rather than reflect on the way in which we live, for most of the time and the patterns, the modes of living are transmitted in varied and often complex ways through what might loosely be called the channels of socialisation. We pick up our culture in the family, at work, at school, through the television and newspaper, through literature, museums and so on, and it is not our present purpose to explore these channels.

What seems to be of greater relevance for the theme of culture and education, is the process of generating and transmitting the more formal and in some sense 'official' or dominant elements of our culture. It is these dominant aspects which become embodied in the ideal or normative concept of culture and the educational system is one vehicle for the transmission of these aspects. The normative culture is contained, partly at least, in the overt curriculum of the schools and in what has come to be called the 'hidden' curriculum. The validity of this norm has long been a matter of . contentious debate which at times becomes highly political.

It is worth considering, therefore, why this is regarded as so important an issue.

2. SOME CULTURAL PRESUPPOSITIONS

I have argued that the concept of 'culture' is an abstraction and in this respect it is similar to concepts such as the

'State' and 'society'. Each concept may be used in an evaluative sense and in turn can command respect and commitment or hostility and opposition. We are aware of them as a force in our lives. They are a part of our 'lived experience' and they help to shape and control us, but we are not sure, or in agreement about what they mean.

In trying to give content to such concepts we draw upon our past experience and on our sense of where and what we are. We also draw upon presuppositions and assumptions which are philosophical in origin. The 'State' may be seen as an overriding concept which transcends all personal ambitions and interests. It controls us and demands allegiance. On the other hand the 'State' can be relegated to a convenience for the protection of individuality, but however we regard it, the State for most of us is the apparatus of political and legal institutions and power, which controls many aspects of our lives. The same might be said of 'culture'. For most of the time, it is a 'given'. We live and work within a cultural framework manifest in institutions, buildings, modes of expression, codes of behaviour, technologies, goals and aspirations. For the most part our culture controls us, yet at various points of conflict and tension, we recognise it as something to be influenced and controlled. This seems to happen when something of importance to us is threatened or devalued. It might be when an ancient building is threatened, when grants to education or the arts are reduced or when freedom of speech or other liberties are threatened. We might also feel threatened by more down to earth issues like the devaluing of our skills and the loss of employment as a result of change in technology.

Implicit in all such issues however, there are presuppositions about our humanity, our individuality and about the nature of social and political relationships.

One basic presupposition is that as human beings we can and should exercise control over our lives. We might disagree profoundly on what should be done in particular cases but we have shared concepts of 'change', 'improvement' and 'progress'. We believe in asking questions, and in considering other possibilities, both of which assume criteria by which to evaluate answers to questions and by which to judge the appropriateness of various courses of action. There is also a predisposition in favour of honesty in asking and answering questions: we have notions about 'truth' and 'truth-telling'. We also value 'rationality' and the giving of reasons both in explanations and in justification of actions. This all presupposes a commitment to living according to rules, at the intellectual level, in our personal relationships and in our social relationships.

'Criteria', 'rules' and 'principles' emerge as fundamental cultural values upon which such ideas as 'skilled performance' and 'intelligent actions' depend. Such ideas derive meaning from our ability to compare performances and to judge them, and this entails the use of criteria, rules and principles according to which judgements are made. Discernment and judgement of this kind enter into most aspects of life including artistic creation, sport, politics, crafts and even such mundane areas as the running of the local bus service. In all such cases, we are accustomed to assessing whether something is good or bad of its kind, efficient or ineffective and so on.

In attempting to identify the abstraction known as our 'culture' therefore, we might begin with the so-called transcendental or presupposed assumptions, ideas and principles which make our way of life possible and which help us to define cultural norms and deviations.

Our culture is also underpinned by a number of ideas about socio-political relationships and although it might be argued that there is no general agreement on what these ideas are, there appears to be a philosophy of individualism implicit in, or at least consistent with our way of life. One illustration of this is to be found in the empirical basis of our conception of knowledge as derived from experience. At an everyday level, the claim to have seen something with our own eyes is often taken as irrefutable, and personal experience often has a higher status than 'academic knowledge'. In its more sophisticated forms, observation and tested experience are part of the foundation of what we call 'science', and both 'observation' and 'experience' are concepts which presuppose the existence of individuals who observe and have experience. Much of our moral thinking rests upon the Kantian argument that the idea of a 'moral' decision presupposes that there are autonomous centres of consciousness and that we cannot be regarded as moral agents unless we are capable of making free choices.

Despite the fact that there are many possible views on social and political issues our liberal democratic tradition embodies a strong individualistic strand which goes well beyond the narrowly political. The early origins of these ideas need not concern us here but a convenient starting point would be John Locke in the seventeenth century for whom the right of individuals to exist was a datum. From this fundamental right he develops a view of government and the State or Commonwealth as a device for protecting individual interests. These ideas have been restated in recent years by John Rawls (1972) and Richard Nozick (1974) into a theory of a minimal State which provides a framework of 'justice' as 'fairness' within which the protection of the rights of individuals is the major goal. The right to choose, is elevated to the status of the supreme 'good' and the logical outcome is a society based upon 'rights' which take precedence over any possible ideas about what might constitute a common 'good'. Indeed, it is assumed that only individuals, in the light of their own interests, can have any conception of 'the good' and this principle is clearly illustrated in the idea of a free market economy based upon resources to individual choices.

It is, perhaps, no accident that this version of individualism is implicit in current government policies designed to reduce State participation in many areas of public life. It can be seen at work in policies on privatisation, the reduction in public funding in education and the arts and in the general idea of a share owning democracy. These policies are not merely the invention of a particular political party or government and in many ways they reflect longer term cultural movements which appear to be producing an increasingly pluralistic society in which consensus on the idea of a 'common good' and on what constitutes a good society, are difficult to achieve. In this respect, therefore, the idea of a culture based on common criteria, rules and principles might be seen as breaking down. On the other hand there are considerable areas in which shared values are evident and criteria, rules and principles re-emerge at sub-cultural levels, and it is this latter phenomenon which helps to generate some of the criticism of present day education and it is to this issue that we now turn.

3. EDUCATION AND CULTURE

It should be recognised that when we use the word 'education' we might have in mind a system, a process or a concept. The extent to which the concept matches up to what actually takes place in practice is important, but we must confine ourselves to a brief consideration of how education seems to be conceived, and especially in relation to the cultural values noted earlier.

In its broadest sense, 'education' has to do with learning, but we can learn things which are considered to be bad as well as those things which are considered to be good. We can learn what is important and that which is trivial, therefore when we begin to conceptualise what education might consist of, we draw upon our cultural beliefs and values in order to determine the 'good', the 'bad', the 'important' and the 'trivial'. We are trying to specify what kinds of learning count as 'education' and by implication we concern ourselves with those aspects of a culture which in some sense 'ought' to be transmitted. Whether or not the 'ought' is an imperative based upon notions of eternal verities, or whether the 'ought' is a question of short term expediency, is an important distinction, which is at the heart of much educational debate.

Education is of importance because it helps to make us what we are. It is not the only influence but it is an important one and as an agency of cultural transmission, 'education' is a form of social control. It helps to identify and legitimate what is regarded as valuable, and the forms of thought and behaviour which one sees as important and acceptable. But perceptions in such matters can vary and there might be conflicting interests and views about the nature of education, which lead us to see it as something which needs to be controlled and the question is 'by whom' and 'by what critieria'? Both governments and individuals have an interest in this question which is essentially about values, but it is also concerned with the exercise of power and this is why education so often becomes a political issue.

One reason why education is a political issue arises from the fact that when the concept of education is embodied in a system and in curricula, a highly selective process takes place. Education does not transmit the whole of the culture. It becomes a filtering mechanism and what emerges may be seen as important or irrelevant, depending upon points of view. Thus since the 1970s governments have emphasised the necessity for education to be directed more specifically to the requirements of technology, and the needs of the economy.

This kind of thinking represents an instrumental conception of education which highlights certain aspects of our culture, namely its preoccupation with material wealth which is of course important. The crucial question is the extent to which wealth creation is singled out for priority and the extent to which it dominates our conception of education. In seeking answers, it is essential to identify the issues at stake. One issue is of course sheer survival, but survival might have other dimensions than the narrowly economic and it might be helpful to compare the two related concepts of 'training' and 'education'.

The concept of 'training', although simpler in some respects than the concept of 'education', is also used in a number of senses which make generalisation difficult. Nevertheless, 'training' typically refers to activities and processes designed to prepare people for specific roles and to develop the performance of specific skills and tasks. We train to do something and for some purpose. In its narrower senses, 'training' may be in the following of drills and routines while at the other end of the spectrum the notions of 'skilled', 'imaginative' and 'intelligent' performances emerge. Thus a highly trained games player might be deemed to display skill in not following standard routines and tactics. In all such cases, however, 'training' suggests fitness of purpose and the overriding aim of training is the attainment of standards of performance for purposes beyond themselves. A stroke in tennis might be aesthetically satisfying but its purpose and its justification is in winning a game. Tools and techniques are mastered because they can be used to make things or to carry out repairs. Training is therefore concerned with ends beyond itself, and skill, understanding and performance are justified if they lead to people being better craftsmen, dentists or teachers and so on. Some skills might be of intrinsic worth, but they need not be in order to come within the concept of 'training'. 'Training' can be for things which are evil as well as for things which are good, and 'training' can also be concerned with tasks that are trivial.

In contrast, the concept of 'education' has normative overtones and we think of the processes of education and achievements within education as being of value apart from any instrumental use. Thus, acquiring knowledge and understanding are regarded as worthwhile as in the development of rational and critical thinking because they are presupposed in our conception of what it means to be human. The ability to ask questions and to judge the validity of answers presupposes such further notions as 'truth' and 'truth telling' as well as an ability to think categorically.

In some senses, such a conception of education implies constraint as does 'training', but it is seen as providing a framework which makes open ended creative thought possible. This is achieved by concentrating on generalisable principles which can be applied in a variety of new situations rather than on specific knowledge to be used in concrete repeatable situations. The ideal therefore is one of learning in order to be liberated from the contingent constraints of the particular here and now. Education is seen as being concerned with the development of autonomous individuals who are able to adapt and to influence their circumstances rather than be constrained by specific roles.

These are, of course, expressions of ideals, but they seem to be the educational counterpart of the general philosophy of liberalism which underlies our culture and which would be at risk if the concept of education and the educational system were very different. We must ask, therefore, whether education should risk being at variance with short term instrumental goals and with governmental policies in order that it should represent more fundamental long term aspects of the culture. A mixture of instrumental training and liberal education is in the end necessary, but in the face of short term problems and pressures, liberal education is less obviously important and more difficult to justify. Liberal education is also potentially destabilising and inimical to political control. A surface manifestation of this is in the tendency for educated people to be more openly critical of governments and to express their own views and opinions. There are, however, indications that the liberal ideal is producing counter tendencies which in the end makes political control easier and this might be the major problem concerning education and the State.

4. THE LIMITS OF INDIVIDUALISM AND THE CONCEPT OF 'PROCESS'

A major tenet of liberal individualism is a denial of the possibility of arriving at a general as distinct from a private, idea of 'the good'. This means much more than the encouragement of individual opinions, especially on matters of social policy. It presumes that there can be no agreement on social policy because individual choice is the primary good. Any attempt to arrive at an overriding consensual 'good' would be a compromise on (conflicting) individual interests, therefore it would impinge the principle of unconditional personal autonomy. By definition, the notion of individual autonomy excludes any higher good because autonomy i̲s̲ the highest good.

The consequence of this view is that not only is the possibility of general agreement ruled out, but its desirability is also denied. There are no criteria by which to judge a general or common good and it is not desirable that there should be any such criteria.

We move logically therefore to a strong version of relativity in social values and there are no general criteria by which to judge actions beyond the criterion of individual choice. The process of choosing thus overrides comparisons between choices and the quality of what is chosen is irrelevant. The liberal ideal of r̲a̲t̲i̲o̲n̲a̲l̲ choice is excluded because of the absence of any valid general criteria by which to judge the rationality of choice.

This view is highly consistent with a consumer orientated technology economy, where the specific nature of technology is secondary to the p̲r̲o̲c̲e̲s̲s̲ of technological development, and w̲h̲a̲t̲ is produced is unimportant. It matters only that something is produced and chosen. No intrinsic value is necessary and that consumers choose to buy, is more important than what they buy. Evaluation of choices at all levels is unnecessary and it gives way to the need for maintaining the processes of choice. What should be a means therefore becomes an end.

The concept of process has entered into much of our thinking. It has been fashionable in education to put 'process before content', in the sense that what is learned, is less important than that something is learned, and the same principle appears to be present in our approach to artistic creation where there seems to be a marked absence of agreed evaluative criteria. The scientific concept of objective knowledge shares similar characteristics in the assumption that knowledge p̲e̲r̲ s̲e̲ is important and here the idea of intrinsic worth is hoisting us on our own petard. It ceases to matter what is discovered or created, and the necessity for moral evaluation of knowledge, discovery and invention is denied. This view has strengths but it also has weaknesses because it obscures the fact that discovery and invention are, in practice, distorted by political and commercial ends which go unquestioned.

Another way of expressing these manifestations is the idealisation of the free market economy which as we have

Culture, Education and the State

noted becomes the epitomy of a process orientated system which actually conceals the fact that consumer choices are dictated by what is made available, and there is little meaningful freedom.

There seems to be a danger therefore that liberal values in the end can become self-defeating in that they actually lead to a reduction in critical evaluation and decision making. It is perhaps no accident that the concept of skill is being devalued by increases in mechanisation where how things are made is subservient to the fact that they are made. With a reduction in skill, there follows a diminution of the concept of skill which is at root 'intelligent discernment' and the whole concept of criteria based behaviour is at risk.

The political consequences should be obvious. There is already a reduction in meaningful political choice and an absence of effective rational debate. The process of political pragmatism has replaced consideration of political principles, and the much vaunted principles behind Thatcherism are reducible to no more than the empty principle of free choice because there is truly 'no alternative'. The liberal society seems therefore to be wide open to transformation to a controlled society as a consequence of having been produced ostensibly by a culture of choice.

In the end, culture and education seem to be irrevocably interrelated both to each other and to politics.

BIBLIOGRAPHY

Arnold, M. Culture and Anarchy 1869 and Cambridge University Press 1932
Eliot, T.S. Notes towards the definition of Culture Faber and Faber 1948
Nozick, R.N. Anarchy, State and Utopia Basil Blackwell 1974
Rawls, J. A Theory of Justice Oxford University Press 1972
Williams, R. The Long Revolution Chatto and Windus 1961, Pelican Books 1965

CONTRIBUTORS

Raymond Banks MA MSc FRSC

Raymond Banks is a Yorkshireman, born and bred in Kingston upon Hull, and educated at Hymers College, Hull and The Queen's College, Oxford. He moved to Nottingham in 1940, where he was employed by the Boots Company in chemical manufacturing and then in the Research Department, until retirement. He is a Justice of the Peace for the County of Nottinghamshire and has served as a Councillor on the Beeston and Stapleford Urban District Council prior to local government reorganisation, from 1946 to 1967. He was Chairman of the Town Planning Committee for the whole of that time, and also Chairman of the South Notts. Joint Planning Committee for many years. He has been Regional Secretary of the National Housing and Town Planning Council since 1948, and Member of the National Executive of that Council. He was National Chairman, 1970-71. He is Hon. Secretary of the Nottingham Civic Society.

Neil Barnes

Neil Barnes was born in 1936. National Service in the RAF was followed by a Sociology degree at Nottingham University where he graduated in 1960. After working for a Market Research Company he joined the BBC Audience Research Department in 1964 and two years later joined the BBC Education Department as a Further Education Officer. He is currently the Chief Assistant to the Controller of Educational Broadcasting.

164

Contributors

John Cain

John Cain was born in 1924. After graduating in Mathematics from London University, followed by three years in the RAF, he taught mathematics and science in secondary schools and colleges in London. In 1961 he became the Assistant Head of Schools Broadcasting for Associated Rediffusion and joined the BBC School Television Department two years later. After a number of senior appointments with BBC Education he became, in 1977, Assistant Controller of Educational Broadcasting, and in 1981, the BBC's Controller of Public Affairs. Following his retirement in 1984, he has been involved part-time researching the history of the BBC.

He is a trustee of Broadcasting Support Services, the charitable trust which provides the public with educational advice and information linked to broadcast programmes, and from 1980-85 was its Chairman.

Kenneth Cooper

Kenneth Cooper took over as Chief Executive of the British Library on 1 September 1984. After reading Modern History at New College, Oxford, he entered the Home Civil Service in 1954, serving in both the Ministry of Labour and HM Treasury. Later he became in turn Chief Executive of the Employment Service Agency and of the Training Services Agency, and was subsequently Director-General of the Building Employers' Confederation. He is currently a member of the Board of the Confederation of Information Communication Industries and Chairman of its Public Affairs Working Party.

Paul E. Fordham

After war service as a 'Bevin Boy' miner in Derbyshire, Paul Fordham graduated in geography from the University of Leeds. He has worked for over 30 years in university adult education in Lincolnshire, Derbyshire and Kenya, where he was the first Director of the Institute of Adult Studies in Nairobi. He is now Professor of Adult Education at the University of Southampton. He is a past Chairman of the National Institute of Adult Continuing Education (England

165

and Wales) and has undertaken extensive consultancy work for the British Council, Commonwealth Secretariat, UNESCO and the International Council for Adult Education.

David Jones

David Jones trained as a painter at the Leeds College of Art and qualified as a teacher at the University of London Goldsmiths' College. From there he went on to teach painting and pottery in the post-school sector before becoming head of an Adult Education Centre in Middlesbrough. He was awarded a Diploma in Adult Education and an MEd by the University of Manchester before joining the Division of Adult and Continuing Education at the University of Nottingham. He is concerned with the training of teachers of adults and his writing and research centre on adult art education and the development of creativity. He has been a member of the Executive and various panels and committees of the Regional Arts Association and is Chairman of the Managers of the Midland Group Arts Centre, Nottingham.

Marista Leishman

Marista Leishman is Director of The Insite Trust. Insite gives professional help to those who work with the public in historic houses, museums, galleries, and all places of interest which attract visitors.

The task of welcoming the public and acting as interpreter on the site calls for skills for which training and support are provided by Insite.

Before starting Insite Marista Leishman was Head of Education in the National Trust for Scotland, having previously worked as the Trust's first Representative in its Georgian House in Edinburgh.

She is married with four grown-up children, and has an MA in English and Philosophy from the University of St Andrews.

Kenneth H. Lawson

Kenneth Lawson is the Assistant Director of the

Contributors

Department of Adult Education at the University of
Nottingham. Having left school at the age of 14 he
subsequently took a Degree in Philosophy, Politics and
Economics at Oxford and he was later awarded a PhD by the
University of Nottingham. He has been the Warden of two
Adult Education Centres. Previous publications include
Philosophical Concepts and Values in Adult Education and
Analysis and Ideology: Conceptual Essays on the Education
of Adults.

John Reeve

John Reeve is Head of Education at the British Museum, and
responsible for the programme of events for the general
public, in-service training for teachers and teachers-in-
training, work with children, schools and colleges; and the
development of learning resources at all levels. He joined
the Museum in 1980, after teaching in comprehensive
schools, and in adult and museum education in Yorkshire. He
holds an MA from Cambridge (History), and Certificate in
Education from Bristol University. He is an author of
children's books and of several articles on multi-cultural
education, learning materials for children, art and design
education in museums etc. At various times he has been a
member of Committees of Association of Art Historians,
Council for British Archaeology, Group for Education in
Museums, and a Regional Examinations Board. In 1987 he
was Adjunct visiting professor at the Hobart and William
Smith College, New York.

Warren Shaw, OBE, MA (Trinity College, Dublin)

Taught in Afghanistan and the Sudan; British Council 1958-
84; serving in Brazil, Nigeria and Germany and as
Representative in Tanzania and Ghana. Co-author of A
Dictionary of the Third Reich (Grafton Books 1987).

Michael D. Stephens

Michael Stephens has been the Robert Peers Professor of
Adult Education at the University of Nottingham since 1974.
He received his PhD from the University of Edinburgh. He

167

has written frequently on the education of adults and been Research Fellow at the Johns Hopkins University, Visiting Scholar at Harvard, Visiting Fellow at Yale, and Japan Society for the Promotion of Science Fellow and Visiting Professor at Kyoto University.

INDEX

Adkins, G. 5, 15
Adult Literacy Campaign
  108
amateurs xi
Annan Committee 104
Archaeological Trust, Trent
  and Peak 124
Archaeology, Council for
  British 121
Architectural Heritage Fund
  116
architecture xi, xii
Arnold, M. 150, 151, 152,
  163
art and design education 73
art galleries x
artist in residence 19
Arts Council x, xiv, 1-23
Athens vii
Australia xiii, 11
award scheme (Nottingham
  Civic Society) 117

Ballinger, Mrs xii
Banks, Ray xi
Barley, Professor Maurice
  119, 121
Beeston and Stapleford
  Urban District Council 115
Beethoven 12

Birmingham Civic Society
  114
Braden, S. 20
Bradley, Thoresby 124
Brand, Ken 127
BBC ix, xi, 25, 94-113
BBC Television for schools
  76
BBC Television historical
  programmes 76-8
British Council ix
  and British colonial policy
  26, 36-7
  direct Government grant
  for 24, 27
  cultural relations of 24-5
  and the Commonwealth 28,
  38-9
  cultural diplomacy of 24,
  34
  English language 27-8, 38
  and British culture 26-7,
  34, 38-9
  ODA 25, 27, 29, 35
  Anglophil institutes 35
  and French colonial policy
  26
  and British colonial policy
  26, 36-7
  role of Representatives 27-

8, 33-6, 38
British history and archaeology 77-9
British Institute of Recorded Sound *see* National Sound Archive
British library xiv, 40-65
British Museum ix, xiv, 65-94, 136
British Museum Library 40, 44-6, 62
British National Bibliography 40-1, 51, 57
Broadcasting Act 1989 98
Bruce, Robert the 131
Building Preservation Institute, Nottinghamshire 128

Callinish Standing Stones 130
Canal, Nottingham and Beeston 123
public access 123
Cardinal of Ferrara vii
Castle, Nottingham 123
excavations 123
green 124
museum 124
tours 127
Castle Gatehouse Shop 124
Castle Road (Little Bins) 126
Caves, Nottingham, Tours 127
Cellini, Benvenuto vii
Celts xii
Central Library for Students 41
Centre 42 18
Chancellor of the Duchy of Lancaster 3, 13, 14
Chardin, Teilhard de 130
China ix-x, xiii, 81-2
Civic Amenities Act, 1967 124

Civic Trust ix, xiii, 113-30
amenity societies 116
associate trusts 116
conference, 1987 128
formation 114
objects 114
services 116
Classical art 74-5
Classical education 74-5
Coates, Professor R.C. 120
Coleridge, S.T. 147
Collin's Almhouses (Abel Collin's Hospital) 119
Cooper, Kenneth x, xiii
Commerce, Nottingham Chamber of 121
community arts 9, 18-20
Concert Hall, Nottingham 122
conservation areas 124
advisory committee 125
Copernicus 134
Council for the Encouragement of Music and the Arts 2
Council of Europe 4, 8, 18
County Hotel, Nottingham 122
Crathes 131, 132
Cromwell, Oliver 123
Cullen, Bob 121, 128
cultural and artistic norms 1
cultural education 1, 94

da Vinci, Leonardo vii
Deare, Cliff 127
Department of Education and Science (DES) 2, 3, 105, 109, 110
Department of Health and Social Security (DHSS) 109
Department of Trade and Industry (DTI) 109, 111
Director-General (BBC) 95
Dorothy Vernon House 119

Index

Drury Hill 122

eastern bypass 120
Eden, Anthony 96
Edinburgh 130
Educational Broadcasting
    Council 111
Eliot, T.S. 150, 151, 163
elitism 140
Elizabeth I (of England) vii
Empire Theatre,
    Nottingham 122
English National Opera 76
English National Opera
    North 10
Environment Week 128
establishment, the 94

Falkland Palace 130
Family First Projects
    Agency 126
Fawdry, Kenneth 106-7
Florence ix
Ford, B. 21
Francis I (of France) vii

Gaelic 100
Glasgow 141-2
Greece xiii
Green's Mill, Nottingham
    126
Gulbenkian Foundation 5

Hamilton, Andrew 123, 126
Hammond, T.W. 114
Hardy, T. 137, 148
Harrison, Margaret 124
Hartlett, E.T. 119
Health Education Authority
    109
Henry, Brendan 120
Heritage Education Group
    116
heritage industry 132, 139
'Heritage Outlook' 128

Hewison, R. 139, 148-9
Home, Extending Your,
    Design Guide 117
Home Improvements, Code
    of Practice 117
Horne, D. 11, 21
housing, high rise 117
Hutchinson, R. 3

India 82
India Office library and
    records 41, 49, 54
Industrial Revolution vii, xii
Inner London Education
    Authority xiii
Insite Trust 130-49
Islamic art 83
Italy viii, xiii

Januszczak, W. 139, 149
Japan 80
Jesson & Son Ltd,
    Nottingham 120
Jinan ix-x
Jones, D. x
Jor, F. 4, 8, 13, 18

Kahn, N. 4, 16
Kelly, O. 8, 9, 20
Kent Opera 76

Lace Market, Nottingham,
    Conservation Policy for
    120
Lambert's Factory, Notting-
    ham 125
Langebach, R. 141, 149
Laws, E.J. 119
Lawson, Kenneth ix, xii
Leeds 10
Leishman, Marista xii
libraries x
Libraries Association
    Library 41
Listener, The 104

Local Education Authorities (LEAs) 108, 111
Locke, J. 157
London x, xiii

Magdalen Street, Norwich 115
Manpower Services Commission (MSC) 109, 111, 126
Market Square, Old, Nottingham (Street Furniture) 126
mosques vii
meetings and visits, Nottingham Civic Society 127
Melbourne xiii
Mennel, S. 4
Metropolitan Museum, New York 69
Middleton, Lord and Lady 128
Milner, M. 136-7, 149
Ministry of Culture viii
Montesquieu, C.L. 152
Moulin, R. 4
multicultural xii
multicultural education 79-88
museums x
museum education 65-93
Museum of Mankind 79, 83, 86-8
music xi

National Central Library 40-1
National Discography 58
National Housing and Town Planning Council 117
National Institute of Adult Education 5
National Lending Library for Science and Technology 40-1
National Preservation

Office 55, 57
National Reference Library for Science and Invention 40
National Register of Microform Masters 55
National Sound Archive 41, 46-7, 50, 58
national values xiv
Natural History Museum 70, 88
Neolithic Revolution xii
Newsletter, Nottingham Civic Society 127
Nicholson, Bill 102
Normanbrook, Lord 98
Nottingham x
Nottingham Civic Society formation 118
Nottingham Guardian-Journal 119
Nottingham University 5
Nozick, R. 157

Office for Scientific and Technical Information 40-1
Open University 101

Pacey, Arnold J. 118
Paolozzi, Eduardo 77, 87-8
parliamentary proceedings televising 97
Patent Office library 40
Patents Information Network 54
private finance xi
projects group, special Nottingham Civic Society 127
publications, Nottingham Civic Society 128

Radio Times 104
Rawls, J. 157, 162
Read, H. 10

Redcliff-Maud Report 4, 6, 7, 8
Reeve, John x, xiii
Regional Arts Associations 6, 14-15, 19, 20
Reith, John 96, 105
Richards, Sir Henry 105
Royal Academy 75
Royal Institute of British Architects 117
Royal Opera House 76
Royal Shakespeare Company 10
Royal Town Planning Institute 117
Ruskin, J. 131, 142, 149
Russell, B. 134, 135, 149
Russell Report (1973) 110, 134, 135, 149

St Mary's Church, Nottingham, floodlighting 126
Scottish Health Education Group 109
Severn, John 127
Shaw, R. 3, 14
Sheriff's Way, Nottingham 120
Shops and Shop Fronts, Design Guide 117
Simpson, J.A. 1, 4, 7-8, 18
South Bank Complex 3
Stonehenge 130
Stratford East 18
Suez Crisis 96

tax concessions viii
Telling, A.E. 121
Theatre Royal, Nottingham 122
'Time for Design' 117
topofilia 140
training 131, 145-8
Treasure Houses of Britain x
Tuan, Y.F. 140-1, 149

United States of America xiii

Victoria and Albert Museum 68-9
Vietnam xiii
visitors surveys 70-2

Walks, Heritage 127
Washington DC ix
Welsh 100
West Germany viii
Wharton, Edith xii
Williams, R. 150, 153, 163
Winnicott, D.W. 138, 142, 149